Funding Social Security

A Strategic Alternative

Funding Social Security contributes to the debate on Social Security reform that is taking place in many countries around the world. This book describes and explains "funded Social Security," a middle position between pay-as-you-go (PAYGO) Social Security and privatized Social Security. Funded Social Security has two distinct components: fund accumulation and portfolio diversification. Funded Social Security uses a mix of payroll taxes and portfolio investment income to finance benefits; the federal government contracts with private investment firms to manage the portfolio of the Social Security trust fund. Like the current U.S. system, funded Social Security is a defined-benefit plan without any individual defined-contribution accounts, so that all risk is pooled; each retiree's benefit (an inflation-adjusted annuity) is linked by a legislated formula to that retiree's own wage history. Funded Social Security differs solely, but crucially, in the *financing* of the system.

Laurence S. Seidman is a professor of economics at the University of Delaware. He previously taught at the University of Pennsylvania and Swarthmore College. Professor Seidman has published articles in the *American Economic Review, Journal of Political Economy, Review of Economics and Statistics, Journal of Public Economics, National Tax Journal, Public Finance Review, Southern Economics Journal,* and the *Journal of Macroeconomics.* His most recent books are *The USA Tax: A Progressive Consumption Tax* (MIT Press, 1997) and *Economic Parables and Policies* (M.E. Sharpe, 1998).

Funding Social Security

A Strategic Alternative

LAURENCE S. SEIDMAN

CAMBRIDGE
UNIVERSITY PRESS

PUBLISHED BY THE PRESS SYNDICATE OF THE UNIVERSITY OF CAMBRIDGE
The Pitt Building, Trumpington Street, Cambridge, United Kingdom

CAMBRIDGE UNIVERSITY PRESS
The Edinburgh Building, Cambridge CB2 2RU, UK   http:/www.cup.cam.ac.uk
40 West 20th Street, New York, NY 10011-4211, USA   http:/www.cup.org
10 Stamford Road, Oakleigh, Melbourne 3166, Australia

First published 1999

Printed in the United States of America

Typeface Times 11/14 pt.   *System* AMS-TEX   [FH]

A catalog record for this book is available from the British Library

Library of Congress Cataloging in Publication Data
Seidman, Laurence S.
Funding social security : a strategic alternative / Laurence S.
Seidman.
p. cm.
ISBN 0-521-65245-6 (hb)
1. Social security – United States – Finance.   I. Title.
HD7125.S524   1999
368.4'301'0973 – dc21   98-41844
                                          CIP

ISBN 0 521 65245 6 hardback

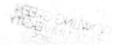

For Jesse and Suzanna

Contents

Contents

Contents

Acknowledgments

I am indebted to the many authors of the articles, books, and reports that are cited or quoted in this book, as well as to the reviewers and editor for their constructive suggestions.

1

Funding Social Security:
An Introduction

An Introduction

Funding Social Security deserves serious consideration in the debate over Social Security reform that is taking place in many countries around the world. Funding Social Security is not a new proposal. Its debt to other reform plans for all its components will be clearly evident from citations and quotes.

Funding Social Security has two distinct essential components: fund accumulation and portfolio diversification. Fund accumulation requires setting tax and benefit rates to achieve substantial annual surpluses. Portfolio diversification is achieved by having the Social Security Administration contract with private firms to invest the Social Security trust fund. Thus, funded Social Security uses a mix of payroll taxes and portfolio investment income to finance benefits, with an important share contributed by each source; for example, investment income might roughly equal payroll tax revenue in a typical year. In its portfolio choice, funded Social Security avoids excessive reliance on either government bonds (because the yield is lower) or corporate stocks (because the risk is higher).

With funded Social Security, all investment risk is pooled: there are no individual accounts. The Social Security Administration contracts with private investment firms (under competitive bidding) to manage the portfolio of the Social Security trust fund; each investment firm manages a share of the trust fund portfolio. Under the contract, each firm must invest its share of the fund in a conservative diversified portfolio of government bonds, corporate bonds, and corporate stocks. The contract with private managers specifies a maximum share for corporate stocks and a minimum share for government securities; for example, the contract might state that corporate stocks cannot exceed half the portfolio, that all stock investment must be broadly diversified, and that government securities must constitute at least a third of the portfolio. Each investment firm

3

manages Social Security's portfolio the way it manages the portfolio of a conservative risk-averse private client; the investment firm handles stock voting as it does for such a private client.

Funded Social Security is entirely a defined-benefit plan without any individual defined-contribution accounts. Each retiree's benefit is linked by a legislated formula to the retiree's own wage history; the benefit is an annuity – an annual benefit that continues for as long as the retiree (or spouse) lives – and is automatically adjusted annually for inflation. If a country (such as the United States) initially has a defined-benefit pay-as-you-go (PAYGO) Social Security system, funded Social Security is achieved by preserving the defined-benefit formula and gradually shifting the financing from payroll taxes to a mix of portfolio investment income and payroll taxes.

Although funding Social Security warrants serious consideration in many countries, this book focuses specifically on the Social Security reform debate in the United States. It is a case study that addresses fundamental issues that are present in most countries considering Social Security reform.

Funding Social Security has two distinct components: fund accumulation and portfolio diversification. To accumulate a large capital fund, taxes and benefits must be set so that Social Security runs annual surpluses: taxes plus fund investment income must exceed benefits. As the capital fund accumulates, its portfolio must be chosen. The funded Social Security plan considered in this book prescribes a diversified portfolio of marketable government securities, corporate bonds, and corporate stocks.

It is crucial to recognize that fund accumulation and portfolio diversification are separate components. It would be possible to have fund accumulation without portfolio diversification: Social Security could accumulate a large fund but invest it solely

4

in special nonmarketable low-yield government securities (as it does under the current U.S. Social Security system). Conversely, it would be possible to have portfolio diversification without fund accumulation: Social Security could maintain only a small fund but invest that fund in a mixed portfolio. In this book, the term *funded Social Security* implies both components: a large capital fund invested in a diversified portfolio.

Fund accumulation is the key to raising the capital accumulation of the economy, whereas portfolio diversification is the key to capturing a larger share of the economy's capital income for the Social Security system. Suppose an increase in the economy's capital accumulation would generate a return to the economy of 6% due to the productivity of the additional physical capital. Fund accumulation without portfolio diversification would raise capital accumulation (provided the balance in the rest of the government budget is unaltered) and generate a 6% return to the economy. If Social Security invests its surplus solely in government bonds earning 2%, then the government would sell fewer bonds to the public and the public would channel more of its savings into private firms, financing additional capital accumulation that generates a 6% return. Portfolio diversification without fund accumulation would not raise the capital accumulation of the economy; if Social Security holds more corporate stocks earning 6% and fewer government bonds earning 2%, then the public will hold fewer corporate stocks earning 6% and more government bonds earning 2%. But fund accumulation *with* portfolio diversification would raise capital accumulation and cause the Social Security system to capture some of the 6% return that is generated by the additional capital accumulation.

There are three important reasons for investing the portfolio in marketable government securities, corporate bonds, and

corporate stocks rather than in special nonmarketable government securities (as under the current U.S. Social Security system). First, the yield on the portfolio will be higher. Second, it
will strengthen the confidence of the public: the status of special nonmarketable government securities is often questioned,
but the status of a portfolio of marketable stocks and bonds is
easily grasped. Third, a marketable portfolio is less vulnerable
to a political raid, because tapping the portfolio involves actual
sale of stocks and bonds rather than the canceling of nonmarketable government securities.

In the United States in 1997, the distinguished Advisory
Council on Social Security (ACSS) provided an important service by submitting to Congress three fundamental reform plans,
each plan supported by a subset of members of the Council.
Three points deserve emphasis. First, the three ACSS plans are
fundamental reforms and are therefore useful vehicles for dis-
cussing the fundamental issues in Social Security; it is for this
reason that this book devotes significant space to the three ACSS
plans. Second, funded Social Security borrows heavily from all
three ACSS plans. Its debt to the authors of these plans will
be clearly evident throughout the book. Third, funded Social
Security nevertheless differs from each ACSS plan.

There are two middle positions between PAYGO defined-
benefit Social Security and privatized defined-contribution
Social Security. One is funded Social Security. The other is
PAYGO Social Security with supplemental individual defined-
contribution accounts. In the U.S. Social Security debate, some
who have sought a middle position favor adding supplemental individual defined-contribution accounts to PAYGO defined-
benefit Social Security. One purpose of this book is to explain
why a second middle position, funded Social Security, deserves
serious consideration.

An Introduction

Under the current U.S. PAYGO Social Security, each retiree receives an annual benefit that is tied to the retiree's wage history by a legislated formula, continues for as long as the retiree (or spouse) lives, and is adjusted annually for inflation. The retiree's benefit varies directly with the wage that person earned as a worker: the higher the average annual wage earned over a person's career, the higher the annual benefit. Benefits are not means-tested, though they are subject to income taxation. Benefits are *partially* redistributive: If worker H earned three times the annual wage of worker L over his career and paid three times as many dollars in payroll tax, then H receives an annual benefit roughly twice as great as L's. Benefits are an annuity: each retiree is paid annually for as long as the retiree (or spouse) lives. The annual benefit has an automatic inflation adjustment.

Like the current U.S. PAYGO Social Security program, funded Social Security is a defined-benefit annuity plan with inflation protection and partial redistribution (from high-wage to low-wage workers). It differs from PAYGO solely in its financing.

In its first four decades (1940–80), the U.S. Social Security system used pay-as-you-go financing: annual payroll taxes from current workers and employers were approximately equal to annual benefits paid to current retirees. The Social Security trust fund was essentially a petty cash fund – only large enough to handle an unexpected shortfall of payroll tax revenue below benefits obligations (determined by the wage histories of current retirees according to a legislated benefit formula). The trust fund did not accumulate significant reserves. Beginning in the mid-1980s, Congress adjusted payroll taxes and retiree benefits to achieve annual surpluses, so that a genuine fund began to accumulate. However, the objective of Congress was to build a temporary fund that would be drawn down to help finance benefits

7

of the Baby Boom generation next century. Thus, the surpluses were viewed as a temporary deviation from PAYGO financing, adopted to handle a temporary demographic bulge. Social Security was expected to return to annual balanced budgets – PAYGO financing – in the long run. Thus, despite the temporary deviation, it is still accurate to view the current U.S. Social Security system as committed to PAYGO financing for the long run.

When PAYGO Social Security begins, its start-up yield (rate of return) is very high because retirees immediately receive benefits even though they paid little or no payroll taxes. The *yield* is a measure of the benefits a person receives as a retiree relative to payroll taxes paid as a worker; the greater the benefits relative to taxes, the higher the yield. The yield on PAYGO Social Security compulsory "saving" (payroll taxes) remains high for several decades because retirees receive benefits over their entire retirement even though they paid taxes over only a fraction of their work career. This high start-up yield is one important reason for the past popularity of PAYGO Social Security. But the longer an individual worker pays taxes over her career, the lower is the yield under PAYGO Social Security.

In the future, most retirees will have paid taxes during their entire work career – the PAYGO system is now mature. Economists have shown that, with steady population and productivity growth and a constant payroll tax rate, the real (inflation-adjusted) yield in a mature PAYGO Social Security program will on average equal the growth rate of real output (approximately the sum of labor force and productivity growth). This is shown in Appendix 2A (of Chapter 2) for a two-period model, and the result holds in a multiyear model (Seidman 1983). According to most long-term forecasts, this growth rate is likely to be about 2% (e.g., 0% for population growth and 2% for productivity growth).

An Introduction

In order to preserve Social Security as a defined-benefit annuity plan with inflation protection and partial redistribution, it may be necessary to gradually fund Social Security: to gradually change its financing from PAYGO to a mix of payroll taxes and portfolio investment income, so that in the future its yield is comparable to the yield available on low-risk private saving. Thus, funding Social Security is a politically *strategic* alternative.

With funded Social Security, its diversified portfolio should on average be able to obtain a return that is several percentage points higher than a portfolio limited to government bonds as well as several points higher than PAYGO Social Security. For example, if the inflation-adjusted yield on a portfolio of corporate stocks is 6% and the yield on government bonds is 2%, then a mixed Social Security portfolio of stocks, corporate bonds, and government bonds would probably achieve a return of 4% with low risk. This 4% return would be twice the 2% return likely to be achieved by PAYGO Social Security.

This 2% gap makes an enormous difference over a person's lifetime. For example, consider a worker of age 45 saving $5,000 that year. Compounded at 2% per year it grows to $7,430 at age 65; compounded at 4% per year it grows to $10,956. Hence, at age 65, the amount is nearly 50% greater ($10,956/$7,430 = 1.47) when the yield is 4% instead of 2%.

Funded Social Security rests on a cautious and realistic view of the stock market. History shows that even a conservative diversified portfolio can perform poorly over a decade. It is important to emphasize two points. First, funded Social Security uses payroll taxes as well as portfolio investment income to finance benefits; it does not put too many benefit eggs in its portfolio basket. Second, the portfolio is conservative: government bonds constitute an important share of the Social Security portfolio,

9

as do corporate bonds; corporate stocks are not only diversified but constitute less than half of the Social Security portfolio.

Like the current U.S. Social Security system, funded Social Security is a defined-benefit plan in which each retiree's benefit is linked to the retiree's own wage history by a legislative formula; the benefit does not directly depend on the performance of the portfolio. If portfolio earnings fall, then a fraction of the portfolio must be sold to finance legislated benefits. However, if the portfolio performs poorly for several years, then either the legislative formula must be adjusted or payroll taxes increased. Thus, indirectly, benefits are eventually affected by portfolio performance; funded Social Security does not eliminate stock market risk. But it does minimize the risk for the individual retiree by (1) pooling the risk over all retirees, (2) utilizing a conservative diversified portfolio invested in government and corporate bonds as well as corporate stocks, (3) spreading the risk over time by selling fund assets as a first resort and adjusting the legislated benefits formula only as a last resort, and (4) using payroll taxes as well as portfolio investment income.

FUNDING SOCIAL SECURITY VERSUS ALTERNATIVE FUNDAMENTAL REFORMS

The aim of this book is to compare funding Social Security with alternative fundamental reform proposals. Although the United States is the case study of this book, the analysis is relevant to other countries contemplating fundamental Social Security reform. Just as the United States is a useful case study, so are the fundamental reform plans proposed by the Advisory Council on Social Security (1997). The ACSS plans represent major reform alternatives, not only for the United States but for many other countries as well.

The Social Security Act requires the Secretary of Health and Human Services to appoint an Advisory Council on Social Security every four years to review Social Security and prepare a report on its review and recommendations. In 1997, the 13-member ACSS issued its long-awaited report. After much discussion and debate, the Council split into three groups offering three different plans for fundamental reform.

One group of six members (Ball, Fierst, Johnson, Jones, Kourpias, and Shea) proposed a maintenance of benefits (MB) plan. The MB plan largely preserves the current defined-benefit PAYGO system, recommends gradually phasing in some modest tax increases, and – most significantly – gives serious consideration to the possibility of the government contracting with private firms to invest a portion of trust fund assets directly in common stocks indexed to the broad market.

Another group of five members (Bok, Combs, Schieber, Vargas, and Weaver) proposed a personal security accounts (PSA) plan. The PSA plan would direct nearly half of the payroll tax (5 percentage points out of the current combined 12.4 percentage points) into a defined-contribution PSA that – like an individual retirement account (IRA) – would be owned by the worker and would be invested in a portfolio of stocks and bonds by a manager chosen by the worker. Thus, the PSA plan privatizes half of Social Security. Its other half would be a simple equal (flat) benefit for all workers with the same years of work (regardless of earnings) financed by payroll taxes.

The remaining group of two members (Gramlich and Twinney) proposed an individual accounts (IA) plan that creates individual defined-contribution accounts as a supplement to the PAYGO defined-benefit Social Security system. The IA plan

11

recommends phasing in tax increases and slower benefit growth, and it proposes a new worker contribution of 1.6 percentage points to be allocated to an individual defined-contribution account. These accounts would be managed by the government but with some portfolio choice given to each worker.

Funded Social Security differs in at least one important respect from each of the three ACSS plans. Like the current U.S. Social Security system, funded Social Security is a compulsory, universal, defined-benefit annuity plan with inflation protection: a retiree receives an annual benefit that is tied to the retiree's wage history by a legislated formula, continues for as long as the retiree (or spouse) lives, and is adjusted annually for inflation. It differs solely, but crucially, in financing.

Funded Social Security has a large permanent capital fund so that its investment income becomes an important source of financing benefits along with payroll taxes. The Social Security fund's broadly diversified portfolio of corporate stocks, corporate bonds, and government bonds is managed by private firms under contract with the Social Security Administration. The contract specifies that the private managers must avoid excessive reliance on either government securities (because the yield is low) or corporate stocks (because the risk is high); in particular, corporate stocks cannot constitute more than half the portfolio, and all stock investment must be broadly diversified. The Social Security capital fund is accumulated by achieving a gap between payroll taxes and benefits during a long transition period, not by government borrowing. The earned-income tax credit is used to protect low-income workers from the transitional tax burden.

How does funded Social Security differ from each ACSS plan? Like the MB plan, funded Social Security is a compulsory, universal, defined-benefit annuity plan with inflation protection

12

and partial redistribution (from high-wage to low-wage workers). The MB plan does envision maintaining a permanent fund that might be invested in corporate stocks and bonds along with government bonds. However, the MB plan proposes accumulating a relatively small fund. By contrast, a central feature of funded Social Security is the accumulation of a large permanent fund so that portfolio investment income becomes as important as payroll tax revenue for financing Social Security. In order to accumulate the large permanent capital fund, there is a gradual temporary payroll tax increase and a gradual temporary slowdown in benefit growth, with protection for low-income workers provided by an expanded earned-income tax credit.

The MB plan authors recommend that Social Security shift from strict PAYGO financing to partial "advance funding" to help finance the retirement benefits of the Baby Boom generation and to contribute in an important way to the long-term financing of the program while improving the return for younger workers. In the ACSS report, however, the MB authors do not propose building a fund large enough to generate investment income equal to roughly half of Social Security benefits. Their emphasis is on "maintaining benefits" rather than on "funding Social Security." Some of the six individuals in the MB group may support funding Social Security – the building of a permanent fund that generates annual investment income comparable to annual payroll tax revenue – but the description of the MB plan in the ACSS report does not include sufficient adjustments in taxes or benefits.

Consider a rough illustration. Today, U.S. Social Security fund assets are almost two times the amount of annual benefits. Under current projections of the Social Security actuaries, the ratio of fund assets to annual benefits will increase gradually to about four over the next two decades and then be drawn down to zero by the end of the third decade. Since benefits are 5% of GDP, suppose that investment income with funded Social Security is eventually 2% of GDP. If the yield on fund assets is 4%, then fund assets must be 50% of GDP, so the ratio of fund assets to benefits equals ten. For example, if GDP is 100 then fund assets are 50, fund investment income is 2, and benefits are 5.

Thus, funded Social Security envisions the gradual accumulation of a permanent fund that is roughly ten times annual benefits; by contrast, the current buildup is projected to achieve a temporary fund that is roughly four times annual benefits at its peak but declines to zero over the subsequent decade. The MB plan envisions preventing the fund from declining to zero, but the description of the plan implies that the annual investment income of its small permanent fund will be much smaller than annual payroll tax revenue. By contrast, with funded Social Security, the annual investment income of its large permanent fund will be comparable to annual payroll tax revenue.

Like the PSA plan, funded Social Security would enable workers to benefit from the higher expected returns of the stock market. However, with funded Social Security, all risk is pooled because there are no individual defined-contribution accounts. Moreover, the Social Security Administration specifies (in its contract with private managers) that excessive reliance on the stock market is not permitted; in particular, corporate stocks cannot exceed half of the portfolio, and all stock investment must be broadly diversified. With the PSA plan, each household would be free to invest its entire portfolio in undiversified corporate stocks. The PSA plan envisions individual defined-contribution accounts that are owned, controlled, and invested by each worker. Funded Social Security is a defined-benefit annuity plan in which the government contracts with private firms to invest its large fund in a broadly diversified portfolio.

An Introduction

The IA plan keeps most of Social Security a defined-benefit annuity plan with inflation protection. Funded Social Security keeps *all* of Social Security a defined-benefit annuity plan with inflation protection. Like the IA plan, funded Social Security prescribes a tax increase and slower benefit growth to build its fund. But while the IA plan retains pay-as-you-go financing for most of Social Security and rejects government contracting with private firms to invest in the stock market, funded Social Security gradually converts the financing of Social Security from PAYGO to a mix of payroll taxes and portfolio investment income. The IA plan introduces small defined-contribution individual accounts to supplement PAYGO Social Security. Funded Social Security fully preserves the current defined-benefit system and does not introduce individual defined-contribution accounts.

Although the ACSS report states that there is little support on the Advisory Council for a significant payroll tax increase, all three ACSS plans in fact contain some tax increase. The transition to funded Social Security calls for gradually phasing in both a modest temporary tax increase and a modest slowdown in benefit growth in order to accumulate the permanent capital fund that will – in the long run – make possible the same replacement rate (ratio of benefit to previous wage) with a much lower payroll tax rate. Low-income workers are given protection from the temporary tax rate increase through the earned-income tax credit.

A final fundamental reform that has been proposed is *means-testing* Social Security. With means testing ("affluence testing"), a retiree with sufficient "means" (income or wealth) would not receive a Social Security benefit. The Social Security benefit would be smaller, the higher is the income (or wealth) of the retiree. The report of the Bipartisan Commission

15

on Entitlement and Tax Reform (1995) considers means testing. Means testing may be viewed as an alternative to funding Social Security because each reform attempts to bring Social Security into long-run financial balance. However, funded Social Security retains the current rough linkage between a person's dollar benefits and that person's past dollar payroll taxes; means-tested Social Security would break that linkage for higher-income retirees.

THE OBJECTIVE OF THIS BOOK

This book quotes and paraphrases many who have written on Social Security reform. Its contribution is to gather their arguments in one convenient place – and to organize those arguments – in order to compare funding Social Security with the other important reform proposals.

This book does not attempt a comprehensive treatment of Social Security reform. It ignores many important Social Security issues treated by other analysts (for example, Ball 1978; Boskin 1986; Munnell 1977; Myers 1993; Steuerle and Bakija 1994). The aim of the book is rather to focus on one central controversial feature of the design of Social Security. It explains the case for funding Social Security by having the government (a) set tax and benefit rates to achieve substantial annual surpluses and (b) contract with private firms to manage its trust fund through conservative portfolio diversification. With funded Social Security, Social Security would remain a defined-benefit annuity plan with inflation protection and partial redistribution.

Funding Social Security is a strategic alternative. In political debate, too often the impression has been generated that

16

there are only two options: Social Security with PAYGO or Social Security with individual defined-contribution accounts. It is crucial that people realize there is another option: *funding* Social Security. Funded Social Security is a defined-benefit plan (without individual defined-contribution accounts) that uses a mix of portfolio investment income and payroll taxes to finance benefits.

2

Funded versus PAYGO
Social Security

Funded versus PAYGO Social Security

This chapter compares funded Social Security with PAYGO (pay-as-you-go) Social Security. They have much in common. Each is a compulsory, universal, defined-benefit annuity plan with inflation protection: a retiree receives an annual benefit that is tied to the retiree's wage history by a legislated formula, continues for as long as the retiree (or spouse) lives, and is automatically adjusted annually for inflation. PAYGO and funded Social Security differ solely in financing.

Funded Social Security has a permanent capital fund that is large enough to make its investment income (along with payroll taxes) an important source of financing benefits. Because it lacks investment income, PAYGO Social Security requires tax revenue roughly equal to benefits. In contrast, funded Social Security requires tax revenue roughly equal to *half* of benefits, because its investment income also equals half of benefits. The capital fund is large enough to make the yield on Social Security saving comparable to the yield on low-risk private saving. The Social Security fund's broadly diversified portfolio of corporate stocks, corporate bonds, and government bonds is managed by private firms under contract with the Social Security Administration. This capital fund is accumulated by gradually opening up a gap between payroll taxes and benefits during a lengthy transition period, not by government borrowing. The expanded earned-income tax credit is used to protect low-income workers from the transitional tax burden.

A DEFINED-BENEFIT ANNUITY PLAN WITH INFLATION PROTECTION AND PARTIAL REDISTRIBUTION

In this book, "funded Social Security" means a defined-benefit annuity plan that differs from the current U.S. PAYGO Social

21

Security program solely in its financing. Each retiree receives an annual benefit that is tied to the retiree's wage history by a legislated formula, continues for as long as the retiree (or spouse) lives, and is automatically adjusted annually for inflation. The retiree's benefit varies directly with the wage that person earned as a worker: the higher the average annual wage earned over a person's career, the higher the annual benefit. The benefit formula is *partially* redistributive: If worker H earned three times the annual wage of worker L over his career and paid three times as many dollars in payroll tax, then H receives an annual benefit roughly twice as great as L's.

With funded Social Security, portfolio earnings and payroll taxes in a given year may be insufficient to finance legislated defined benefits while maintaining the fund. Legislated defined benefits must be paid despite any short-term fall in earnings and taxes. To accomplish this, fund assets – stocks and bonds – may be sold to supplement earnings and taxes. If the discrepancy persists over several years, so that fund assets decline significantly, then either (a) payroll taxes must be raised to restore sufficient capital to the fund or (b) the formula that links a retiree's benefit to the retiree's wage history must be changed by explicit legislation. Thus, a defined-benefit plan, whether PAYGO or funded, cannot provide a guarantee that a given wage replacement rate (the ratio of the benefit to the preretirement wage) will always be maintained. However, a defined-benefit plan makes the wage replacement rate independent of any short-term fall in earnings and taxes. Moreover, any change in the replacement rate is made explicit, as a last resort, and with advanced warning to retirees.

Before contrasting PAYGO and funded Social Security, it is useful to emphasize their common feature: both are defined-benefit plans. By contrast, a defined-contribution Social Security plan would vary benefits with short-term variations in the fund's investment income. This is obvious under privatized Social Security with individual accounts. But a defined-contribution Social Security plan could be implemented with a single collective fund. Each retiree would receive a benefit that varies with short-term fluctuations in the fund's investment income, investment risk would be pooled, and each retiree's benefit would be a specified share of the fund's earnings rather than an amount linked to her own wage history by a legislated formula.

With defined-contribution Social Security, the risk of stock market fluctuation would be borne by retirees collectively. By contrast, with funded Social Security, the risk of stock market fluctuation is borne initially by nonretirees through the immediate sale of fund assets required to pay benefits linked to past wage histories. Some stock market risk is still borne by retirees, because eventually there may be a legislated change in the benefit formula if the stock market continues to stagnate.

A shift from the current defined-benefit Social Security to a defined-contribution Social Security would therefore shift most of the risk from the general population to retirees. Diamond (1997) argues in favor of Social Security's maintaining a defined-benefit system rather than switching to a defined-contribution system:

> Interest rate risk, both at the time of annuitization and during the accumulation process, is put squarely on the individual retiree in a defined contribution system. Interest rate risk does not disappear just because one has a defined benefit system. Rather, it is dealt with by

adjustment in taxes or in the benefit formula when the cumulated outcomes are sufficiently far from the projection implicit in the design of an actuarially balanced system. . . . Ideally, benefit formulas are moved gradually and with considerable lead time. A large defined benefit system, such as Social Security, is capable of responding this way. . . . A large trust fund makes it easier to adapt smoothly to changing circumstances. . . . The economics of well-designed systems are clear: defined benefit systems have greater ability to smooth interest rate risk over successive cohorts of retirees . . . . (p. 38)

It is important to distinguish between defined-benefit Social Security and a defined-benefit plan at a single business firm. At such a firm, a defined-benefit plan has several serious shortcomings. First, a worker who leaves the firm before retirement usually loses his pension benefit. Second, the person must work for that specific firm for a designated number of years to qualify for any benefit. Third, if the firm experiences financial trouble or goes out of business, the worker's pension may be in jeopardy. These shortcomings have understandably spurred the recent growth of defined-contribution plans in the private sector.

None of these serious shortcomings apply to defined-benefit Social Security. First, a worker need not worry about losing benefits by leaving a particular firm. Second, as long as the person is employed somewhere in the market economy for a reasonable period, the person qualifies for Social Security benefits. Third, the financial fate of any particular firm does not jeopardize a worker's benefit. Thus, a defined-benefit Social Security plan is free from the serious disadvantages of a defined-benefit plan at a single firm.

24

Funded versus PAYGO Social Security

THE YIELD ON SOCIAL SECURITY SAVING

With funded Social Security, financed by a mix of payroll taxes and portfolio investment income, the *yield* (rate of return) depends on the return generated by the Social Security portfolio of government bonds and corporate stocks and bonds. In turn, the yield on corporate stocks and bonds depends over the long run on the marginal product of real capital. Business firms issue stocks and bonds to finance the purchase of real capital – machinery, equipment, and technology – which raises the output that the firm can generate. This increase in output generated by an additional dollar of real capital is the "marginal product" of capital. A conservative estimate for the real (inflation-adjusted) yield on a funded Social Security portfolio is roughly 4%.

When PAYGO Social Security begins, its start-up yield is very high because retirees immediately receive benefits even though they paid little or no payroll taxes. The yield is a measure of the benefits a person receives as a retiree relative to payroll taxes paid as a worker; the greater the benefits relative to taxes, the higher the yield. The yield is defined as the discount rate that makes the present value of a person's benefits as a retiree equal the present value of the person's taxes as a worker. The greater are benefits relative to taxes, the higher is the yield.

Economists have shown that, once a PAYGO system is mature (so the typical retiree has paid taxes over his entire work career), if there is steady population and productivity growth and a constant payroll tax rate then the real yield in a PAYGO Social Security program will on average equal the growth rate of real output (approximately the sum of labor force and productivity growth). This is shown in Appendix 2A for a two-period

25

model; it holds also for a multiyear model (Seidman 1983). According to most long-term forecasts, this growth rate is likely to be about 2% (e.g., perhaps 0% for population growth and 2% for productivity growth).

FELDSTEIN'S 1975 ARTICLE

In a path-breaking article, Martin Feldstein (1975), professor of economics at Harvard, proposed the conversion of PAYGO Social Security to funded Social Security. Although Feldstein currently favors privatized Social Security (Feldstein 1996), it is instructive to consider carefully his 1975 article.

Feldstein argued that the pay-as-you-go financing of Social Security reduces real capital accumulation. With PAYGO, payroll taxes finance consumption by retirees instead of real investment by business firms. Yet most workers quite rationally view payroll taxes as compulsory saving that will yield benefits in retirement; in response, they therefore reduce their own voluntary saving. As a consequence, each year there is significantly less real investment in plant, equipment, and new technology.

Feldstein's assertion about the magnitude of the impact on voluntary saving has been challenged. Using econometric techniques, Feldstein and other researchers have arrived at varying estimates of the impact of PAYGO Social Security on saving. But it seems likely that the impact is substantial. Suppose for a moment that there were no Social Security program. Perhaps a 25-year-old would not save more. But anyone over 40 would surely be aware of the plight of a 65-year-old who failed to save adequately, and most would try to avoid this fate. Although the magnitude of the impact may be judged uncertain, it seems

26

likely that Social Security has had a significant adverse effect on saving.

Mindful of political pragmatism, Feldstein (1975) asked:

> How then should the current Social Security program be reformed to reduce the harmful effects on capital accumulation? And can this be done without the public hostility and political opposition that might be aroused by a major restructuring of the benefits? Fortunately, it is possible to alleviate the problem without making any changes in the structure of the program that would be noticed by the general public. (p. 88)

Feldstein gave this answer: Gradually accumulate a large Social Security capital fund. In the terminology of this book, gradually convert PAYGO Social Security to funded Social Security. He explained:

> If a substantial portion of Social Security taxes were instead saved and invested by the government, as they would be in a private pension program, the Social Security system would accumulate its own reserves, which would offset the reduction in private capital accumulation. Stated somewhat differently, the Social Security program, by collecting more in taxes each year than it paid in benefits, would add to the national rate of saving and would thus partially offset the reduction that it causes in the private savings rate. (p. 88)

Feldstein then responded to various objections. Will a Social Security fund raise real capital accumulation even if its portfolio

27

is limited to government bonds? Yes, because those who sell their government bonds to the Social Security fund will invest their receipts in corporate bonds and stocks. Will a Social Security fund require excessive interference with the private economy? No, because the fund can invest in government bonds, private mortgages, and corporate bonds, so that there is no need for owning equity shares in private companies. Feldstein did not comment on the possibility of having the Social Security Administration contract with private firms to manage its portfolio. In what follows it will be argued that private management of the portfolio would enable investment in a diversified portfolio of corporate stocks as well as bonds while avoiding political interference. How will the annual surplus be achieved? Feldstein replied:

> Accumulating a surplus in the near term requires raising the Social Security tax rate. This is seen by some as unfair or excessively burdensome. It must be remembered, however, that the Social Security tax is already scheduled to increase substantially in the future in order to deal with the changing demographic structure of the population. By raising the tax rate now, the eventual total increase can be reduced, since the interest income of the Social Security fund will be available to pay part of the cost of future benefits. If we do not raise the tax rate now, we will be placing an unfair burden on the next generation – asking them to pay a much higher tax rate to support us than the rate that we charged ourselves. And if they refuse to shoulder this burden, and tax themselves more heavily than we are now taxing ourselves, the benefits that we receive will be very much smaller than we now expect. (p. 91)

But is it acceptable to have the Social Security administration responsible for a large fund? Feldstein replied:

> Finally, there are some critics who object to lodging such a fund in the Social Security agency rather than in the Treasury or in some other government department. I recognize that there is no compelling economic logic for assigning this responsibility to Social Security. But historically and politically, the Social Security system has been viewed as a substitute for private savings and private pensions. The Social Security agency is therefore the natural place in the government structure in which to locate a public savings or pension fund. Adding to the already existing Social Security fund should raise none of the ideological or political objections that might be aroused by the creation of a new government agency. It is not just a coincidence that in other countries the ownership of a large public capital fund has been specifically vested in the Social Security agency. (p. 91)

FELDSTEIN'S 1996 ARTICLE

In his 1996 Richard T. Ely lecture to the American Economic Association, Feldstein remains concerned about capital accumulation. But he also emphasizes a second argument in favor of funding Social Security. He argues that funding Social Security will result in a much better deal for workers than PAYGO Social Security: it will achieve a much higher yield on workers' compulsory saving (payroll taxes) and thereby enable a much smaller payroll tax to achieve the same retirement benefits. Although Feldstein now favors funding Social Security

29

by privatizing it, he agrees that his numerical illustrations apply equally to both funded Social Security and privatized Social Security.

Feldstein notes that a mature PAYGO Social Security program will on average yield a real (inflation-adjusted) return equal to the normal growth rate of real output, which is currently about 2.6%. He contends that Social Security with full funding would achieve a real return equal to the marginal productivity of real capital, which Feldstein estimates to be 9.3%.

Feldstein then presents a simple example to illustrate the consequences for an individual saver. He points out that, under Social Security with PAYGO and a 2.6% real return, an employee age 50 must contribute $1,000 to yield $1,900 at age 75, whereas under Social Security with funding and a 9.3% real return, the same employee would need to contribute only $206 to yield the same $1,900 at age 75. This means that, in the long-run, Social Security with funding can yield the same retirement benefits for a much smaller payroll tax rate than Social Security with PAYGO.

In this example, the required tax rate would be only about 20% ($206/$1,000) as high as the current tax rate; instead of the current combined (employer plus employee) payroll tax rate of 12.4%, this example implies a combined payroll tax rate of only about 2.5%. Although moving from PAYGO to funding (while maintaining benefits) requires an initial increase in the tax rate, in the long run it enables a substantial cut in the payroll tax rate to only about 20% of its current level.

Feldstein concedes that the yield on Social Security with funding will vary more than the yield on Social Security with PAYGO. To allow for the greater risk, he estimates that the appropriate return to compare to PAYGO's 2.6% might be 6.4% instead of 9.3%. In this example, the implication is that a 50-

year-old must contribute $403 to obtain $1,900 at age 75. Adjusting for risk, the required tax rate with funding would be only about 40% ($403/$1,000) as high as the tax rate with PAYGO; in the long run, it enables a combined payroll tax rate of only about 5.0%, roughly 40% of its current level of 12.4%.

Thus, Feldstein advocates funding Social Security for two distinct reasons. In his 1975 article he emphasized that funded Social Security would yield higher capital accumulation than PAYGO Social Security. In his 1996 article, he also emphasizes that Social Security with funding would be a much better deal for workers than Social Security with PAYGO: it would yield a much higher real return on their compulsory saving and thereby enable a much smaller payroll tax rate to achieve the same retirement benefits. Although his 1996 article indicates that Feldstein favors funding by privatization, his example applies equally well to funded Social Security.

THE CASE FOR RAISING THE NATIONAL SAVING RATE

The Social Security capital fund is accumulated by setting taxes above benefits during the transition, not by government borrowing. This is necessary to achieve an increase in the national saving rate and the capital stock in the long run; this point is emphasized by Aaron, Bosworth, and Burtless (1989). Financing the fund accumulation by government borrowing would cancel the positive impact on the saving rate and capital stock. The earned-income tax credit should be used to protect low-income workers from the transitional burden, but other workers and some retirees must share the burden from the initial slower growth in consumption that accompanies the increase in the national saving rate.

Is it desirable to raise the national saving rate? Some would argue against it by pointing out that, even with the current saving rate, future generations will enjoy a higher standard of living than today's population. Why sacrifice more today to further raise the standard of living in the future? In response, we consider first a traditional and then a novel economic argument for raising the national saving rate.

The traditional economic argument is that our current saving rate is not the result of preferences being expressed in an undistorted free market. Saving has been discouraged by two government interventions: the taxation of capital income under our income tax, and PAYGO Social Security. One remedy for the first is to convert the income tax to a progressive consumption tax (Seidman 1997). One remedy for the second is to convert PAYGO Social Security to funded Social Security.

The novel economic argument is that there are at least two "public goods" relating to saving that will be inadequately supplied in a free market: (1) poverty reduction for low-skilled people willing to work; and (2) our contribution to the "ascent of humanity" through technological progress. With standard public goods like national defense, without government intervention many individuals would "free ride" and wait for others to contribute; hence too little national defense would be financed. Similarly, many people surely value reducing poverty for people willing to work as well as advancing the well-being of humankind through technological progress. Yet without government intervention, many people would free ride and wait for others to save more. This fact gives another justification for government encouraging a higher saving rate through tax reform and Social Security reform.

Any increase in the saving rate has a transition cost. Even if phased in gradually to avoid recession, the attendant reduction in the consumption rate causes slower consumption growth than would otherwise occur. For example, instead of growing 2.6% per year, consumption might grow only 1.6% per year for half a decade. Although consumption growth remains positive, below-normal growth entails a short-run sacrifice. Both the traditional and novel economic arguments suggest that the long-run gain outweighs the short-run loss. Further discussion is given in Seidman (1997, 1998b).

Clearly, the objective of reducing poverty for low-skilled workers would be undermined if such workers were burdened with the transitional increase in payroll taxes. But this can be prevented by using the earned-income tax credit (EIC). One purpose of the EIC, enacted in the mid-1970s, is to offset the burden of payroll taxes on low-income workers. The EIC can thus be used to offset the burden on these workers of the transitional increase in payroll taxes that accompanies funding Social Security.

THE CASE FOR RAISING THE YIELD ON SOCIAL SECURITY SAVING

Some defenders of PAYGO Social Security argue that the yield on Social Security saving is not very important. But they may underestimate the importance of the yield in maintaining public support for a compulsory Social Security program. The high start-up yield of PAYGO Social Security is gone forever, and we are now entering a permanent situation where PAYGO Social Security will (on average) have a lower return than other forms of saving. As this fact is gradually absorbed by the public, it is likely that support for a compulsory PAYGO Social Security program will erode. Many young workers may lobby to get out of Social Security because they correctly perceive that they can achieve a higher return on other forms of saving. That PAYGO Social Security commanded strong public support during its first few decades is no guarantee that this support will remain once the public realizes it no longer has a high yield.

Substantial erosion of popular support might eventually lead to a phase-out of Social Security, where obligations are met to those who paid payroll taxes in the past but workers are then free to save as they choose, and welfare benefits only are provided for those who fail to provide adequately for their old age. This gradual termination of Social Security has its advocates and will be discussed in Chapter 3. But if one believes that relying on welfare would be inferior to Social Security, then we should give a high priority to raising the yield on Social Security saving so that it once again has a high enough yield to retain broad public support.

FUND ACCUMULATION VERSUS PORTFOLIO DIVERSIFICATION

Fund accumulation is the key to raising the capital accumulation of the economy, while portfolio diversification is the key to capturing a larger share of the economy's capital income for the Social Security system. Feldstein (1975) explains:

> I have learned from experience that proposals for the establishment of a large Social Security trust fund are

often met with various incorrect objections. . . . It is often alleged that accumulating a Social Security fund would not add to real capital accumulation. . . . Consider what actually happens when the Social Security program has a surplus with which it buys outstanding government securities on the open market. . . . The private individuals who originally sold their government bonds to the Social Security fund will invest the proceeds in private bonds and stocks. [Footnote: This assumes that the government does not undo the achievement of the Social Security fund by increasing its general deficit.] This additional demand for private securities will increase the funds available for private investment, and extra private investment increases the real capital stock and raises future income. (pp. 89–90)

Barry Bosworth of the Brookings Institution makes the same point:

Much of the discussion of full funding versus pay-as-you-go financing has been skewed by an excessive focus on the government bond rate as the relevant measure of the rate of return on a funded system. While that rate is appropriate for evaluating the financial condition of a Social Security fund that limits investments to government securities, it is not at all appropriate for measuring the benefits to the nation or future generations. The Social Security fund earns a 2% return because it opts to invest in risk-free government securities; but in buying government securities, it frees up resources that pass through capital markets and can be used by others who are willing to invest in riskier forms of capital earning a

higher rate of return. In particular, if the saving of Social Security, the excess of its tax and interest income
above outlays, ultimately adds to national saving, it can
finance an increase in physical capital.... The result
is an estimate of 6.2% for the real return on the capital
employed in the domestic economy. (1996, p. 98)

Henry Aaron of the Brookings Institution writes:

It seems only fair that Social Security reserves be managed so that beneficiaries have the same investment opportunities as private savers do. It also seems fair that
Social Security beneficiaries receive returns on their
payroll taxes that reflect the benefits to society resulting from Social Security reserve accumulation. Let's be
clear on one fact. Each extra dollar of saving earns the
same return whether it is saved privately or through Social Security. Private saving makes that dollar available
directly for private investment. The social gain is the
private rate of return. Adding a dollar to Social Security reserves reduces federal borrowing from the public
by a dollar, leaving an extra dollar of private saving for
private investment. The social gain from adding to Social Security reserves is, again, the private rate of return.
Unlike private pension funds, Social Security reserves
cannot be invested in private securities. The prohibition
means that Social Security will pay smaller benefits than
private pensions can pay for each dollar of tax or contribution although the social returns to both forms of
saving are identical. The differential guarantees invid-
ious comparisons with returns on private savings and
thereby jeopardizes long-term public support of social

insurance. Lifting the prohibition [would remedy this].
(1997, p. 21)

Portfolio diversification without fund accumulation would
not raise the capital accumulation of the economy; if Social Security holds more corporate stocks earning 6% and fewer government bonds earning 2%, then the public will hold fewer corporate stocks earning 6% and more government bonds earning
2%. But fund accumulation *with* portfolio diversification would
raise capital accumulation and allow the Social Security system
to capture some of the 6% return that is generated by the additional capital accumulation – provided the balance in the rest of
the government budget is unaltered.

THE YIELD ON STOCKS, BONDS, AND CORPORATE CAPITAL OVER THE LONG RUN

The portfolio of funded Social Security contains a mix of corporate stocks, corporate bonds, and government bonds. Currently,
the U.S. Social Security trust fund is restricted to holding a special nonmarketable government bond. Funded Social Security
does not go to the opposite extreme of excluding government
bonds. It prescribes a diversified mix of marketable government bonds, corporate bonds, and corporate stocks. Moreover,
funded Social Security uses payroll taxes as well as portfolio
investment income to finance benefits. Thus, it should be emphasized that funded Social Security does not rely excessively
on the stock market. However, since the most controversial
new component of Social Security financing would be corporate stock (equities), we will focus on this component.

37

Funding Social Security

In *Stocks for the Long Run,* Jeremy Siegel (1994), a professor of economics at the Wharton School of the University of Pennsylvania, provides a history of the yields of stocks and bonds. Note the phrase "long run" in the title. Siegel focuses on the performance of stocks over periods of several decades and longer. In the next section we cite evidence, consistent with Siegel's evidence about long-run performance, that implies caution about the performance of stocks in the short run – where "short run" is one or even two decades.

Although writing at the time of a rising stock market, Siegel takes account of stock market plunges. He begins with a magazine quote in the summer of 1929 from John Raskob, a top executive at General Motors, advocating a $15 monthly investment in stocks as the way to wealth in an interview entitled "Everybody Ought to Be Rich." In September 1929 the Dow-Jones industrial average hit a historic high of 381. In late October the stock market crashed. In the summer of 1932, the Dow-Jones average was 41; it had lost nearly 90% of its value. Shouldn't this financial calamity teach us to stay away from the stock market? Siegel notes that the conventional wisdom is that Raskob's recommendation was foolish and typifies the irrational mania that periodically grips Wall Street.

But Siegel challenges the conventional wisdom. He asserts that if someone listened to Raskob and consistently put $15 per month into stocks, after only four years he would have been ahead of someone who put the same money into Treasury bills. After 30 years, his stock portfolio would have yielded an impressive 13% return on invested capital, far exceeding the returns earned by conservative investors who abandoned stocks at the market peak and shifted into Treasury bonds. People who never bought stock, citing the Great Crash as their reason, eventually fell far behind investors who steadily accumu-

38

lated equity. Siegel concludes that even the Great Crash did not undermine the superior performance of stocks as long-term investments.

Siegel's assertion is provocative. The proposal to have Social Security invest in the stock market is often met with a warning about the Great Crash of 1929. That experience is certainly good reason to avoid excessive reliance on stocks. Funded Social Security relies half on payroll taxes and half on portfolio investment income, and stocks are less than half of its portfolio (at least a third must be government bonds). But if Siegel is correct then it is still worth having a conservative diversified mix of stocks as one component of financing Social Security. In the short run, of course, a stock market plunge would compel Social Security to sell government bonds in its portfolio in order to pay the benefits it owes retirees. But if Siegel is correct, Social Security would still be better off with a mix of payroll taxes and a diversified portfolio (containing corporate stocks as well as corporate bonds and government bonds) than it would be with sole reliance on payroll taxes.

Siegel reviews the historical data from 1802 to 1992. He focuses on total returns – the returns that are generated by capital gains and the reinvesting of interest and dividends. He reports that the total return on equities is higher than the return for all other assets. He says that bear markets, and even the crash of 1929, are overwhelmed by the long-term upward trend.

It appears that there is a strong case for the funded Social Security portfolio to hold an important share in diversified stocks rather than to limit its holdings to government or even corporate bonds. But the next important question is whether such a portfolio is likely to generate a significantly higher real (inflation-adjusted) yield than PAYGO Social Security. Recall that, after the Baby Boomers are gone, PAYGO should yield a real return roughly equal to the growth rate of real output (perhaps 2% in the coming decades).

Siegel notes that, in the 1950s and 1960s, stocks were usually viewed as a good hedge against inflation, but in the 1970s the fall in the stock market weakened this view. Inflation seemed harmful to stocks. Although stocks were often poor short-term hedges, Siegel says they have been excellent long-term hedges against inflation. He reports that, over the past two centuries, the average real (after-inflation) compound return on stocks has been 6.7% per year. Moreover, in the major subperiods, real returns on stocks have been 7.0%, 6.6%, and 6.6%, respectively, showing stability and persistence. Thus, Siegel reports that the long-run real return on stocks has been about 4 percentage points higher than what can be expected from PAYGO Social Security in the future. Obviously, this is a very large differential.

But could a Social Security portfolio do almost as well by holding corporate bonds instead of stocks? Siegel says that while the real return on stocks has remained stable, the real return on both short-term and long-term bonds has dropped significantly over time. In the nineteenth century, the real return on bonds and bills was substantial. He reports that the real annual return on bills has fallen from 5.1% to 3.2% to a bare 0.5% since 1926, while the real annual return on long-term bonds has fallen from 4.8% in the first subperiod to 3.7% in the second to only 1.7% in the third. Siegel states that one must go back 150 years, to the period 1831–61, to find any 30-year period for which the return on either long- or short-term bonds exceeded that on equities. Thus, for more than a century, stocks have clearly outperformed fixed-income securities for long-term investors.

In his concluding chapter, Siegel offers advice to the individual investor. His advice would surely be relevant to the managers of the Social Security portfolio. He recommends investing in a highly diversified mutual fund. Such a fund offers investments called *index funds,* which yield returns extremely close to those of the major market indexes, such as the Standard & Poor's (S&P) 500 index. By holding a large number of stocks, such a fund is able to match overall market performance with extremely low costs. This investment strategy is sufficient to achieve the superior returns that have been achieved through stocks over the long run.

Another approach to assessing the prospects for a Social Security portfolio invested partly in corporate stocks is to examine data on the profitability of corporations. Presumably, over the long run, the yield on stocks is influenced by the profitability of corporations. One such study is by Feldstein, Dicks-Mireaux, and Poterba (1983). They explain that their procedure is to define total capital income as the sum of corporate interest payments and corporate profits (with a capital consumption adjustment and inventory valuation adjustment); then the rate of profit is the ratio of this measure of total capital income to the replacement value of the corporate capital stock (defined to include fixed capital, inventories, and land). The authors use estimates of economic depreciation and of the replacement cost of fixed business capital constructed by the Department of Commerce. They report that, for the 32-year period 1948–79, the total pretax rate of return averaged 11.5%.

Two other studies provide more recent estimates. Poterba and Samwick (1995) find a value of 9.2% for the real pretax rate of return on capital in the nonfinancial corporate sector for the years 1947–95; they estimate 8.5% for a more recent period when they ignore property taxes paid by corporations. A study by Rippe (1995), who has worked with Feldstein on similar studies, provides an estimate using similar methodology to the study just cited. He finds that, from the highs in the mid-1960s (in the 13%–14% range), the pretax return fell into the 5%–7% range in the early 1980s. But it has since risen, so that from 1990 to 1994 it has averaged 9.3% (in 1994 alone it reached 11.0%). Over the whole period 1953–94, the average was 9.6%.

It must be recognized, however, that the corporate income tax drives a wedge between the pretax return to capital and the after-tax return that is received by investors. As Feldstein (1996) concedes in his reference to Rippe's estimate of 9.3%, individuals do not earn the full 9.3% pretax rate of return because individual retirement accounts and private pension plans earn a return that is reduced by federal, state, and local corporate taxes. Because those taxes averaged 42% of the pretax return (Rippe 1995), Feldstein estimates that the real net yield available to savers has been about 5.4%. He notes that a funded retirement system could deliver the full 9.3% pretax return to each individual saver by rebating the corporate taxes.

Without rebates on corporate taxes, the return actually received by the corporate stocks in a Social Security portfolio will on average be roughly 6%, not 9%. Still, with funded Social Security, a Social Security portfolio that is broadly diversified in stocks, corporate bonds, and government bonds should be able to achieve an average return that is several percentage points higher than a portfolio limited to government bonds as well as several points higher than PAYGO Social Security. For example, if the inflation-adjusted yield on a portfolio of corporate stocks is 6% and the yield on government bonds is 2%, then a mixed Social Security portfolio (of stocks, corporate bonds, and government bonds) would probably achieve a return of 4% with low risk. This 4% return would be twice the 2% return likely to be achieved by PAYGO Social Security.

This 2% gap makes an enormous difference over a person's lifetime. For example, consider a worker age 45 saving $5,000 that year. Compounded at 2% per year this sum grows to $7,430 at age 65; compounded at 4% per year it grows to $10,956. Hence, at age 65, the amount is nearly 50% greater ($10,956/$7,430 = 1.47) when the yield is 4% instead of 2%.

CAUTION CONCERNING THE STOCK MARKET

Caution against excessive reliance on the stock market is given in a study by the U.S. General Accounting Office (1998) entitled *Social Security Financing: Implications of Government Stock Investing.* This GAO report states:

> Historically, the rates of return on stocks have exceeded interest rates on Treasury securities, although stock returns are more variable. According to an analysis prepared for the Advisory Council [on Social Security], real yields on stocks – i.e., adjusted for inflation – have averaged about 7%. In its deliberations, the Advisory Council agreed to use this rate in estimating average future yields on stocks. Of course, an average return over a long period of time obscures the reality that stock returns fluctuate substantially from year to year. . . . According to the analysis by the Congressional Research Service, although the 30-year moving average of the S&P 500 since 1970 consistently outperformed the Treasury returns credited to the Social Security trust fund, the 10-year moving average of the S&P 500 under performed the trust fund's Treasury returns at times . . . . (pp. 39–40)

The GAO report presents a table showing the best and worst returns on large company stocks for varying investment periods from 1926 through 1996. The report comments:

> Given that from 1926 to 1996, there was no 20-year period with a negative [nominal] return, an investor might reasonably expect to earn a positive [nominal] return over 20 years. . . . There is no guarantee that investing in the stock market, even over two or three decades, will yield the long-run average return. (pp. 40–1)

FUNDED SOCIAL SECURITY AND
THE FINANCING MIX

Funded Social Security uses a mix (roughly half and half) of payroll taxes and fund portfolio investment income to finance benefits, in contrast to PAYGO Social Security which uses only taxes. It can be argued that a mix is preferable to relying solely on portfolio investment income or solely on taxes. On the one hand, the return through portfolio investment income should on average exceed the return through PAYGO by several percentage points. On the other hand, even a conservative, diversified portfolio of government bonds, corporate bonds, and corporate stocks is subject to risk. Over certain time periods, the return through investment income may well fall below the return through PAYGO. Consider a period when employment and payrolls grow normally but the stock market plunges. In such a period, PAYGO will do better than the portfolio. Of course, there will be other periods when employment and payrolls grow normally but the stock market soars. In such a period, the portfolio

44

will do better than PAYGO. In a great depression, employment, payrolls, and portfolios all collapse. But it seems likely that the variation in payroll growth will usually be smaller than the variation in portfolio growth. Thus, risk aversion calls for a mix of financing.

The optimal mix of portfolio investment income and payroll taxes is hard to assess with precision, but there is no urgency about pinpointing the optimal mix. Like many other countries, the United States is now essentially a PAYGO system (with a temporary fund accumulation to help with the retirement of the Baby Boomers). To spread the burden over many decades, which may be necessary for political feasibility and fairness, the fund should be accumulated very gradually by slowly widening the gap between payroll taxes and benefits. Over decades, the share of portfolio investment income will grow slowly and the share of payroll taxes will decline slowly. Experience during this lengthy transition should prove helpful in assessing the best mix for the long run.

THE IMPORTANCE OF EXCLUDING SOCIAL SECURITY FROM OFFICIAL BUDGET REPORTS

Although Social Security is currently "off-budget," it is nevertheless included in official reports concerning the federal budget and official assessments of whether the budget is balanced. Because Social Security has been running annual surpluses since the mid-1980s and should continue to run surpluses at least through 2010, its inclusion in official budget reports makes the budget look better. For example, suppose the Social Security surplus is $100 billion and the rest of the budget has a deficit of

$100 billion. Congress and the president will announce that the budget is balanced.

The public favors a balanced budget and focuses on the official budget report to judge how Congress is doing. In this example, if Social Security is excluded then the public will judge that Congress still has a $100 billion deficit to eliminate; if Social Security is included, they will judge that a balanced budget has been achieved. Clearly, excluding Social Security will create greater pressure on Congress to balance the rest of the budget.

One purpose of converting Social Security from PAYGO to funding is to raise the national saving rate. This purpose would be defeated if an increase in the Social Security surplus by $100 billion permitted Congress to increase the deficit in the rest of the budget by $100 billion. If this happens, the increase in Social Security saving would be canceled by the increase in rest-of-government dissaving, so that national (private plus government) saving would stay constant. If Congress is required to balance a budget that excludes Social Security then any increase in Social Security saving will not be canceled by an increase in the deficit in the rest of the budget. Thus, funding Social Security together with exclusion from the official budget should raise national saving.

Funded Social Security merits separation from the official budget. Although it is compulsory, its payroll tax is earmarked for Social Security and its rate will eventually be much lower than today's rate because roughly half of its benefits will be financed by earnings on a portfolio of stocks and bonds. Neither its tax nor its portfolio earnings should be available to finance other government programs. The best way to protect its integrity is separation from the official budget.

Barry Bosworth (1996) of the Brookings Institution explains the importance of excluding Social Security. If Social Security is an integral part of the total budget, he argues, then it is doubt-ful that a surplus in the fund would actually lead to a rise in national saving. If funding Social Security is to succeed in rais-ing national saving, there must be a change in the budgetary process to clearly differentiate Social Security from the oper-ating budget of the government. He reports that most states present their budgets in ways that exclude their retirement pro-grams. As states have built up their pension reserves, they have usually been able to resist the temptation to increase their own borrowing as an offset. Bosworth suggests that the best practi-cal approach would be to remove Social Security revenues and expenditures from the budget documents used by Congress in its work on the budget.

The six MB members of the ACSS (Ball, Fierst, Johnson, Jones, Kourpias, and Shea) make the argument for exclusion in the context of advocating serious consideration of stock mar-ket investment of the Social Security fund. They believe that the budget should be used for allocating government income among programs during the budget period, whereas Social Security – with its benefit commitments spread over decades – requires a long-range framework. Social Security, like the retirement sys-tems of the states, should be outside the allocation goals of the short-term budget cycle (while remaining subject to review, of course, as part of the government's long-range planning). Dis-cipline is imposed on Social Security by using a 75-year time frame; after all, the Council and others are currently concerned with an imbalance that does not arise for some 30 to 35 years. If Social Security were off-budget in actual practice, it would be easier to plan the annual budget and easier to plan for Social Security's long-term needs.

Although the public may support a complete separation of Social Security from the rest of the budget, Congress and the president may resist such separation because it will make "balancing the budget" more difficult. Nevertheless, funding Social Security should increase the chance of excluding Social Security from budget assessments. If Social Security is funded and accumulates a portfolio of stocks and bonds that is managed by private investment firms, then it will look less like an ordinary government program and more like a private pension. Funding Social Security therefore makes it more likely that Social Security will be treated as a separate pension plan and thereby be excluded when evaluating whether the federal budget is balanced.

THE FEASIBILITY OF MANAGING A
SOCIAL SECURITY PORTFOLIO

The case for feasibility can be inferred from a book by Francis Cavanaugh (1996), the first executive director and CEO of the Federal Retirement Thrift Investment Board and the senior career executive responsible for debt management policy advice in the Treasury Department during the 1980s. It should be pointed out that (i) Cavanaugh believes that the problem posed by the retirement of Baby Boomers can probably be handled by relatively minor adjustments in PAYGO Social Security, including the fund buildup launched in the mid-1980s, and (ii) he does not directly state whether he prefers PAYGO Social Security (with a temporary fund to help with the Baby Boomers) or funded Social Security (with its permanent fund to help with the financing of Social Security benefits even after the Baby Boomers are gone). But it is instructive to cite his chapter on Social Security because of his views and experiences relevant to the feasibility of managing a Social Security portfolio.

48

Funded versus PAYGO Social Security

Cavanaugh writes that there is a need to reconsider the investment policies of the trust fund because the policy of running surpluses, instituted in 1983 (in anticipation of the retirement needs of the Baby Boomers), has made investment earnings much more important. The recent development of stock index funds provides an acceptable vehicle for the investment of public funds in private equity securities. Cavanaugh points out that the federal government has historically followed an unusual portfolio policy by investing only in its own securities. There are approximately 800,000 private (insured and noninsured), state, and local government pension funds, and more than one third of the assets in these funds has been invested in the stock market; about half of the assets in private noninsured funds are corporate stocks. Cavanaugh concludes that the best practical way to increase the Social Security fund's earnings significantly is to invest a substantial portion of it in the stock market. He then gives a remarkable personal anecdote:

> As a U.S. Treasury Department economist and public debt manager, I was frequently asked to respond to proposals to invest the Social Security or other government funds in the stock market. We opposed such proposals for the following reasons: (1) government ownership and control of private corporations (a.k.a. socialism) are incompatible with our free-enterprise economy and would raise serious conflicts of interest for public officials, and (2) stocks are too risky an investment for public funds. Treasury testimony before Congress in 1988 contained the following statement on the specific question of investing the Social Security trust funds in the stock market: "Aggressive movement of the funds into equities and other private securities would entail higher

risk of loss or default than Treasury obligations, a risk unsuitable to the social policy goal of the programs. If ownership of equities or private sector bonds were contemplated, significant problems would arise as to potential federal control of corporations, the allocation of investment resources, and the conduct of business. We recommend against such involvement." (pp. 100–1)

But Cavanaugh goes on to make the following important point:

These problems can now be avoided by investing in broad stock index funds so that the government's interest in any particular corporation in the index is relatively small and indirect. Prohibiting the government from voting the stock avoids the problem of government control. While individual stocks or sectors of the economy may well be unacceptable risks for government funds, a broad stock index fund provides the relative safety of diversification. Although the stock market is volatile in the short run, the experience of the past fifty years shows that this volatility is not a serious risk for long-term investments, such as retirement funds. (p. 101)

He then relates his personal experience as follows.

Accordingly, in 1986 the Congress authorized stock index fund investments (without voting rights) by the Federal Retirement Thrift Investment Board, which administers the Thrift Savings Plan for federal employees. As the first executive director of the board (1986–1994), I encountered no significant problems as we selected an

index (the S&P 500), obtained competitive bids from
large index fund managers, and established a highly efficient stock fund with minimal administrative expenses.
By 1996, 1 million federal employees had elected to invest $13 billion in the board's stock index fund. I see
no reason why the Social Security trust fund should not
have the same stock investment advantage as the Thrift
Savings Plan. (p. 101)

It should be noted that the Thrift Savings Plan is a defined-
contribution (rather than a defined-benefit) plan. Hence, it
promises retirees the earnings of its portfolio rather than a benefit tied to the retiree's wage history. But the important point for
our purpose is Cavanaugh's judgment, based on his own experience, that it is feasible to contract with private firms to manage
a broadly diversified Social Security portfolio.

Index investing was formerly available only to institutional
investors, such as pension fund managers. Then, in the mid-
1970s, indexed mutual funds became available to individual
investors (for example, the 500 Portfolio of Vanguard Index
Trust). Since then, index investing has become an increasingly
popular strategy. Indexing tries to match the investment returns
of a specified stock or bond market benchmark, or index. The
portfolio manager tries to replicate the investment results of the
target index by holding a representative sample of the securities in the index. Indexing is a passive investment approach that
emphasizes broad diversification and low portfolio trading activity. It appeals not to investors who expect to make a "killing"
but rather to long-term investors who seek a competitive investment return through broadly diversified portfolios.

Index investing illustrates one feasible method of managing
a Social Security portfolio. Of course, index investing does not

guarantee a positive return; the whole stock market can fall. It would therefore be prudent for funded Social Security to hold an important share of its portfolio in low-risk government bonds.

Peter Diamond of MIT has written extensively about Social Security during the past two decades. He emphasizes the significance of index funds for Social Security:

> It is now straightforward for an investor, even one as large as Social Security, to invest while having little say about the allocation of capital in the economy. The innovation that is central for this possibility is the growth of mutual funds, particularly index funds. Index funds hold a fraction of the shares of all the firms that make up some index, such as the Dow-Jones average, the Standard and Poor's index, or, for that matter, all the firms traded in a particular stock exchange. No one seems to think that the Social Security trustees should be picking good investments. Rather, passive investment into indexes is considered to be both prudent fiduciary behavior for the trustees, and the government behavior desired by people fearing poor investment policies. (1996a, pp. 229–30)

Diamond (1997) cites the Thrift Savings Plan (TSP) of federal employees as a successful example of insulation from politics. However, he admits that TSP is a defined-contribution plan and that, under a defined-benefit system, retirees may have less direct financial stake in protecting the funds.

> Nevertheless, with a doubly insulated structure; a board of trustees that has considerable independence, fiduciary responsibility, and limited powers; and a political

culture that endorsed the principle that Social Security should be protected from political interference for unrelated purposes, the risk of political interference in investment choice would not seem to be large. (p. 42)

Diamond concedes that state government defined-benefit systems for government employees have been less successful than the TSP in avoiding political interference, but he argues that the fact that Social Security is a universal program should generate more vigorous monitoring by citizens.

The six MB members of the ACSS (1997) support some buildup of the Social Security fund ("partial advanced funding") and state that serious consideration should be given to investing nearly half of the fund in the stock market. These MB (maintenance of benefits) members do not recommend a buildup nearly as large as funded Social Security, nor are they definitely committed to stock market investment of the fund. But their arguments in favor of serious consideration of stock market investment are relevant to the case for funded Social Security.

They write that it is reasonable for Social Security to have the same freedom to invest part of its funds in the broad equities market in the same way as other pension funds, both private and public. The principle of investment neutrality would be established by law, requiring investment solely for the economic benefit of Social Security participants and not for any other economic, social, or political objective. An expert board would be established (similar to the Federal Retirement Thrift Investment Board, which administers the Thrift Savings Plan for federal employees). The board would choose an appropriate passive market index (such as the Russell 3000 or the Wilshire 5000); select, through competitive bidding, several index portfolio managers with experience in managing large institutional accounts;

monitor portfolio management; and periodically recommend changes in the index or in portfolio managers. The MB advocates then emphasize an important distinction between a funded defined-benefit Social Security and a defined-contribution Social Security:

> It is very important not to confuse the idea of investing in an indexed, passively managed portfolio of equities with proposals to move toward a system of compulsory individual savings accounts. Under the first approach, Social Security remains a defined-*benefit* plan; under the second it is converted in part to a defined-*contribution* plan, with benefits determined not by law but by individual experiences with investment. (p. 85)

The six MB members continue:

> Investment in stocks by a defined-benefit plan is not, of course, a new idea, nor does it fundamentally alter the nature of a public plan. State retirement systems with defined benefits invest heavily in stocks – but are still public plans. As Social Security's trust funds build up in anticipation of future costs, it simply makes good sense to consider investing part of the buildup in stocks in order to obtain a higher return than is possible under a policy of investment only in low-yield government obligations. . . . We reiterate that except for this change in investment policy, Social Security's principles and structure would remain unchanged under this approach. Social Security continues as a defined-benefit plan, with the amount of benefits and the conditions under which

they are paid still determined by law rather than by individual investments. (pp. 83–6)

Henry Aaron of the Brookings Institution has written several books on Social Security and is a former chairman of the Social Security Advisory Council. His view (1997) is similar to the six MB advocates of the ACSS. He notes there is some fear that lifting the current prohibition on investment in corporate stocks would result in pressure on trustees to make politically motivated investments. He points out that managers of the Federal Employees Retirement System and the pension funds for the Federal Reserve System and the Tennessee Valley Authority – all of which invest in private securities – have remained entirely independent in their fund management. He suggests, as an additional safeguard, that Congress might establish an organization, modeled on the Board of Governors of the Federal Reserve System, to manage the Social Security trust fund and its investments. He argues that even though experience in other countries demonstrates that governments may interfere with those who manage monetary policy or who supervise investment of public and private pension funds, in the United States independence has been achieved in monetary policy and can also be achieved for the management of a Social Security capital fund.

PROTECTING THE SOCIAL SECURITY FUND FROM A RAID

What is to prevent Congress and the president from raiding the fund at some future time, drawing it down to pay benefits? Defenders of PAYGO financing argue that this question illuminates a decisive advantage of PAYGO. They point out that Social Security was initially intended to accumulate a large fund, but that political pressures resulted in the tapping of the fund after only a few years and in the conversion to PAYGO financing. They contend that, because any fund is likely to be tapped, it is sensible not to try to build such a fund.

The potential tapping of the fund is a serious concern. However, it should be recognized that Social Security since the mid-1980s has succeeded in building up a significant fund. This recent experience provides some evidence that it may be politically possible to accumulate and preserve a Social Security fund.

There are at least four ways to reduce the chance of a raid. The first step has already been taken: the Social Security Administration has been given greater independence from Congress by being made an independent agency. Second, as discussed previously, Social Security should be excluded from all official reports of the federal budget. Treating it as a separate agency with a separate budget should enhance its independence.

Third, the fund should hold a portfolio of corporate stocks, corporate bonds, and government bonds that are traded in the open market. By contrast, today's Social Security fund is restricted to special nonmarketable government bonds that seem equivalent to mere bookkeeping entries at the Treasury. As a result, much of the public is confused about whether today's Social Security program has accumulated genuine assets. If the Social Security portfolio held the same assets as private portfolios, this confusion would disappear. Moreover, a raid on the fund would involve the actual sale of corporate stocks, corporate bonds, and government bonds in the open market and would therefore be hard to conceal and easy for the public to comprehend.

Fourth, each worker can be sent an annual statement that provides an estimate of her retirement benefit. The key to deterring a raid is to make sure that current workers realize that it is their future benefits that are being raided. If the fund is drawn down then its investment income will be lower in future years, eventually compelling a cut in legislated Social Security benefits. If the Social Security Administration sends each worker an annual estimate of her retirement benefits (based on current tax rates, benefit rules, and the size of the fund and its investment income), then a raid on the fund this year would reduce each worker's estimated benefit in next year's annual statement. Any member of Congress who votes for a raid would know that workers in the home district would soon learn the impact of this vote on their own projected dollar retirement benefit.

The annual statement would be a good thing in itself. Today, most workers have little idea of how much to expect from Social Security. An annual statement is worthwhile just to help people figure out how much they need to save for retirement. Yet the statement would also be an obstacle to a congressional raid on the Social Security fund.

THE TRANSITION

Funding Social Security entails a gradual phase-in of a modest temporary payroll tax increase and a modest temporary slow-down in benefit growth (with low-income workers protected by expanding the earned-income tax credit). Then, as the investment income of the fund grows, the tax rate is gradually reduced to a lower permanent level and the replacement rate is gradually restored to its initial level.

Diamond (1997) explains that the essential element of accumulating a large fund is taxing present workers to benefit future workers. This makes Social Security financially more valuable to future workers at a cost of making it less valuable to those who pay the tax to build the trust fund. He notes that it is the accumulation of the large fund, rather than portfolio choice, that imposes the burden.

There is no way to escape the transition cost if the objective is to raise the national saving rate through the funding of Social Security. Raising the saving rate entails a short-run cost in order to achieve a long-run gain. In this case, the cost is borne as a combination of a temporary tax increase and a temporary slowdown in benefit growth. This fact applies to privatized as well as funded Social Security. There is a trade-off. The faster the fund is accumulated, the sooner are gains achieved but the greater is the cost borne by today's adult population. Conversely, the slower the fund is accumulated, the later are gains achieved but the smaller is the cost borne by today's adult population. The low return that would be received by today's workers during the transition to funded Social Security is emphasized by Geanakoplos, Mitchell, and Zeldes (1999).

There have been several simulation studies of the transition from PAYGO to Social Security with funding. Most of the models have envisioned funding through privatization. However, it is reasonable to interpret the results of these studies as also applying very roughly to conversion to funded Social Security. This interpretation is based on the assumption that, with funded Social Security, each individual acts roughly as though she has a privatized fund equal to her share of the aggregate fund. Simulations based on this assumption provide a rough first-pass estimate of the impact of funding Social Security.

Kotlikoff (1996) simulates the transition path to Social Security with full funding using a version of the life-cycle growth model described in Auerbach and Kotlikoff (1987). In the initial PAYGO steady state, the real (inflation-adjusted) rate of return to capital is about 9%; in the fully funded steady state, it is about 7% (the higher capital / labor ratio reduces the marginal product of capital and hence the real rate of return on capital). In the simulation, there is an immediate reduction in the payroll tax to zero and a schedule that gradually phases down the PAYGO Social Security benefit over many years. Most simulations have a schedule with a 10-year delay (to protect current retirees) followed by a 45-year benefit phase-down, so that each age cohort receives roughly the benefit to which it is entitled based on the payroll tax it has previously paid. Three alternative ways to finance these benefits during the phase-down are simulated: an income tax, a consumption tax, and borrowing. Kotlikoff reports that the utility (measured in wealth equivalents) of those born after funding is about 10% higher than before funding. Those working in the economy when funding begins experience a small rest-of-life loss; the largest loss for any age cohort is about 2% of rest-of-life utility.

Kotlikoff, Smetters, and Walliser (1998) simulate the transition path to Social Security with funding using an enhanced version of the Auerbach–Kotlikoff life-cycle growth model. As in Kotlikoff (1996), the simulations have a schedule with a 10-year delay and then a 45-year phase-down. This model includes heterogeneous earning classes within each age cohort. The authors report that privatization would yield welfare gains for all future workers. In the long run, utility (measured in wealth equivalents) would rise 8% for average earners, 6% for the poorest agents, and over 4% for the richest agents. The loss for those in the economy when funding begins, as well as the pattern of loss across earning classes in a given age cohort, depends on the method of financing the transitional PAYGO benefits; but, as in Kotlikoff (1996), the largest loss is generally about 2% of rest-of-life utility.

Funding Social Security

Feldstein and Samwick (1997) simulate the transition path to Social Security with full funding using data and forecasts for the U.S. economy. They assume a real rate of return on capital of 9%. The simulation assumes that Social Security must pay benefits earned by taxes paid in the past under PAYGO while simultaneously accumulating an aggregate fund that will eventually replace PAYGO financing. In the simulation, the payroll tax rate is raised for roughly two decades, but the increase is surprisingly modest. Beginning at 12.4%, the combined payroll tax rate is immediately raised by 2 percentage points to 14.4%, its peak, and then is gradually phased down. It drops back to 12.4% in two decades, 9% in three decades, 6% in four decades, and converges to a permanent value of only 2%.

Although the initial increase in the tax rate is modest, middle-aged and older workers are a bit worse off because the tax rate is a bit higher than 12.4% for about two decades. Young workers, however, are better off because the much lower tax rate after two decades outweighs the slightly higher tax rate of the first two decades. All future workers are much better off, as the tax rate phases down to 2%. Feldstein and Samwick make the interesting point that the loss to middle-aged and older workers is less than the gain to their children, so that virtually all nuclear families are net gainers.

The Feldstein–Samwick simulation, however, assumes a real (inflation-adjusted) return of 9%. They justify this figure as follows.

> The use of a 9% real rate of return deserves further comment. The real pretax rate of return on capital in the nonfinancial corporate sector can be estimated by comparing the sum of interest, dividends, retained earnings and all corporate taxes to the replacement value of the

capital stock. For the years 1960 through 1994, this averaged 9.3%. [Footnote: See Rippe (1995). Poterba and Samwick (1995) found a value of 9.2% for the years 1947 through 1995 and of 8.5% for the more recent period when they ignored property taxes paid by corporations.] A 9% real pretax rate of return is also consistent with the long-term portfolio returns with which most of us are more familiar. A portfolio of 60% equity and 40% debt (essentially the financing ratio of nonfinancial corporations) had a yield of about 5.5% over both the postwar period and the period since 1926. Since corporation taxes at the federal, state, and local level take approximately 40% of pretax debt and equity income (Rippe 1995), a portfolio return of 5.5% of income corresponds to a pretax real return of about 9%. (p. 120)

Their simulations assume that the full 9% return can be captured by investors (by a rebate of the estimated corporate taxes). They ignore any decline in the return that should follow an increase in the capital/labor ratio of the economy. Although they recognize that the 9% must be adjusted downward several points for risk, their main simulation results use 9%. Hence, their results probably understate the transitional burden and overstate the long-run gain.

By contrast, Seidman and Westenbroek (1998) simulate fund accumulation using a 4% real return. They use all of the assumptions used by the Board of Trustees of the Federal Old-Age and Survivors Insurance and Disability Trust Fund in its annual report (1998) except one: the rate of return. The 1998 annual report uses only a 2.8% real return (a 6.3% nominal return and a 3.5% inflation rate), which is appropriate given the report's assumption that the Social Security portfolio is invested entirely in special nonmarketable government securities. It seems plausible to assume that a portfolio of marketable government bonds, corporate bonds, and corporate stocks would obtain a real return of at least 4%. Thus, Seidman and Westenbroek use a 7.5% nominal return, given the report's assumption of a 3.5% inflation rate.

Their simulations are of a partial equilibrium nature: the authors ignore the impact of fund accumulation on the payroll tax base. If fund accumulation raises capital accumulation in the economy then it should also raise the capital/labor ratio, the marginal product of labor, and the real wage of workers, so that the next century's payroll tax base should be higher (and the return to capital, lower) than the 1998 report projects. Thus, the Seidman–Westenbroek results probably overstate the transitional burden and understate the long-run gain.

In their base simulation, the combined employer–employee payroll tax rate is set 1.0% above its currently projected value in the year 2000: 13.4% instead of 12.4%. In 2005, it is set 2.0% above, and in 2010, 3.0% above, where it remains until 2040; then it is reduced to 2.0% above in 2040, 1.0% above in 2045, its baseline value in 2050, 1.0% below baseline in 2055, 2% below in 2060, and 3% below in 2065, where it remains through 2075. Benefits are unchanged until 2015. In 2015, the ratio of benefits to taxable payroll is reduced to 1.0% below baseline; it remains at that level until 2050, when it is returned to its baseline value.

With these tax and benefit schedules and a real return of 4%, the ratio of fund assets to annual benefits rises from 2.5 in 2000 to 8.9 in 2025, 12.4 in 2050, and 9.8 in 2075, so that (in the long run) the ratio of fund assets to annual benefits is about 10. Fund investment income as a percentage of total income (payroll taxes plus investment income) rises from 11% in 2000 to 38% in 2025, 55% in 2050, and 58% in 2075; hence, in the long run, investment income is over half of total income. By contrast, the 1998 report projects a peak ratio of fund assets to annual benefits of 3.2 in 2012. Fund investment income as a percentage of total income peaks at 18% in 2015. The fund is projected to reach zero by 2033.

In another study, Seidman and Lewis (1998) simulate the very gradual funding of Social Security in a general equilibrium life-cycle growth model; the model incorporates the impact of capital accumulation on wage and the payroll tax base (as well as on the return to capital) and is similar to a model used by Seidman (1986) to study a gradual phase-down of Social Security. Although the model does not attempt a high degree of empirical accuracy, plausible parameter values are utilized. In the initial PAYGO Social Security steady state, the payroll tax rate is 15%, the replacement rate (the ratio of the Social Security benefit to the wage in the economy) is 45%, and the real rate of return on capital is about 8%. In the final funded steady state, the same 45% replacement rate is achieved with a tax rate of about 4%, and the real rate of return on capital is about 6.5% (the higher capital/labor ratio reduces the marginal product of capital and hence the rate of return on capital). Fund investment income is about four times as great as payroll tax revenue. Three fourths of fund inflows are paid out as benefits, while one fourth is retained so that the Social Security capital fund grows at the same rate as national income.

In this example, PAYGO is gradually phased out over three generations (90 years). In year 0, a schedule is enacted. After a 15-year delay, there is a gradual phase-down over the next 75 years of the PAYGO payroll tax rate and the corresponding PAYGO benefit. Thus, PAYGO financing ends after 90 years. At the same time, there is a gradual phase-in of the funded payroll tax rate from year 0 through year 45. In this example, the highest combined payroll tax rate occurs in the year before the PAYGO phase-out begins and equals about 16% – just 1 percentage point higher than its initial value of 15%.

During the transition, many age cohorts experience a small decrease in rest-of-life utility. In this example, the retirees in year 0 are largely protected by delaying the beginning of the phase-out of PAYGO benefits to year 15. But age cohorts in the work force (ages 20 through 65) in year 0 experience a small decrease in rest-of-life welfare. However, everyone who will enter the work force within a few years will enjoy a gain in lifetime welfare. A new entrant (at age 20) to the labor force will have roughly the same rest-of-life utility, but that person's child, grandchild, and all future cohorts will be significantly better off in the funded Social Security economy than they would have been in the PAYGO economy. In light of these simulations, it seems sensible to convert from PAYGO to funded Social Security very gradually over several generations.

CRITICISMS OF FUNDED SOCIAL SECURITY
BY PAYGO ADVOCATES

Criticisms of funded Social Security by advocates of individual accounts will be given in Chapter 3 on privatization and Chapter 4 on supplemental individual accounts. Here we concentrate on criticisms by PAYGO advocates.

PAYGO advocates worry about reliance on the stock market. They argue that even though the stock market has performed well over the long run, persons who retire when the stock market is down would be in trouble. There have been several periods since the Great Depression when the stock market has stayed down for over a decade. It is therefore too risky to place too many retirement eggs in the stock market basket.

In response, it must be emphasized that funded Social Security does not put most retirement eggs in a stock market basket. Advocates of funded Social Security can make several counterpoints. First, funded Social Security would use a mix of payroll taxes and portfolio investment income; payroll taxes would continue to contribute an important share of the financing. Second, the firms that manage the Social Security portfolio would be required to select a conservative, diversified portfolio with a significant share of government bonds and corporate bonds in addition to corporate stocks; the contract would specify a maximum portfolio share for corporate stocks and a minimum portfolio share for government bonds (e.g., a maximum of half for corporate stocks, and a minimum of a third for government bonds). In this book, the return on this conservative portfolio has been estimated to be only 4%, several points lower than estimates given for a portfolio consisting solely of corporate stocks.

Third, funded Social Security (like current Social Security) is a defined-benefit plan. Each retiree's benefit depends on the retiree's wage history according to a legislated formula. A fall in the stock market has no immediate effect on retiree benefits. True, if the stock market stays down for several years, investment income will have to be supplemented by the sale of fund assets in order to finance the benefits prescribed by the legislated formula; and if the stock market stays down long enough, Congress will have to raise payroll taxes or revise the benefit formula.

But it is important to contrast this response of funded Social Security with the response of a defined-contribution plan. Under a defined-contribution plan, retirees receive whatever the fund has accumulated. If the stock market drops, benefits are reduced immediately. As long as the stock market stays down, benefits stay down.

Thus, the PAYGO advocate is right to worry about excessive reliance on the stock market. As we will see in Chapter 3, this worry is indeed relevant to privatized Social Security, where each household is free to choose its own portfolio and receives whatever that portfolio earns. The worry is less relevant to funded Social Security, where all investment risk is pooled, payroll taxes remain important, each retiree's benefit is linked to his wage history by a legislated formula, and the Social Security Administration specifies that its fund be invested in a conservative diversified portfolio that includes not only corporate stocks but government and corporate bonds as well.

PAYGO advocates worry about a raid on the fund. They point out that Social Security was originally intended to be funded but within a few years was converted to PAYGO. Congress decided to tap the fund to pay benefits to current retirees. PAYGO advocates fear that any fund accumulated for current workers will be prematurely raided to pay benefits to current retirees. Thus, it is better to accept this political reality and rely on PAYGO financing.

A potential raid is a problem for funded Social Security. However, several points should be noted. First, pressure to raid the fund was significant in the 1930s because of the plight of the elderly during the Great Depression. Hopefully, that economic calamity will not be repeated. Second, Social Security has successfully accumulated a significant fund during the past decade and a half. Third, four measures can be used to reduce the chance of a raid: (1) maintain the independence of the Social Security Administration; (2) exclude Social Security from the federal budget that must be balanced; (3) invest the Social

Funded versus PAYGO Social Security

Security fund in a portfolio of stocks and bonds that must actually be sold in the open market in order to implement a raid; and (4) send an annual statement of projected benefits to current workers.

APPENDIX 2A: THE YIELD ON PAYGO
SOCIAL SECURITY

The yield on PAYGO Social Security saving can be illustrated with a simple example. Assume there are two equal-length life stages: work and retirement. Each person works in stage 1 and retires in stage 2. In period 1, assume each worker earns a wage of $5,000 and pays a 20% payroll tax of $1,000. What will a worker receive as a benefit in period 2 upon retirement? Because PAYGO Social Security runs a balanced budget, the benefit in period 2 will depend on the tax revenue collected in period 2.

Initially, assume that productivity (output per worker) equals the wage and that productivity stays constant, so the wage stays at $5,000. With 100 workers, in period 1 output is 100 × $5,000 = $500,000. Then in period 2, with the same 20% tax rate, each worker again pays $1,000 in tax. But suppose there is a 50% increase in the number of workers and thus a 50% increase in output (150 × $5,000 = $750,000, which is 50% more than $500,000). Then, in period 2, there are 100 retirees and 150 workers. Hence, in period 2, the tax revenue collected is 150 × $1,000 = $150,000 and the benefit per retiree is $150,000/100 = $1,500. A worker who paid a tax of $1,000 in period 1 and receives a benefit of $1,500 in period 2 obtains a return on Social Security saving of 50% (= ($1,500 − $1,000)/$1,000). Note that the return equals the

67

growth rate of output, 50%, which equals the growth rate of labor when productivity stays constant.

Instead, suppose that the number of workers stays constant at 100 but that productivity – output per worker – grows 50% (from $5,000 to $7,500), so there is again a 50% increase in output ($100 \times \$7,500 = \$750,000$, which is 50% more than $500,000). Because the wage increases 50% from $5,000 to $7,500, with a 20% tax rate the tax per worker increases 50% from $1,000 to $1,500. In period 2, the tax revenue collected is $100 \times \$1,500 = \$150,000$ and the benefit per retiree is $\$150,000/100 = \$1,500$. Once again, a worker who paid a tax of $1,000 in period 1 and receives a benefit of $1,500 in period 2 achieves a return of 50% on Social Security saving. This return equals the growth rate of output, 50%, which equals the growth rate of productivity when labor stays constant.

Finally, suppose instead that labor and productivity each increase 50%. Output increases to $150 \times \$7,500 = \$1,125,000$ in period 2, a 125% increase over its value of $500,000 in period 1. Note that the growth rate of output (125%) equals the sum of the growth rates of labor and productivity (50% + 50%) plus the product of the growth rates (50% × 50% = 25%). Because the wage increases 50% from $5,000 to $7,500, with a 20% tax rate the tax per worker increases 50% from $1,000 to $1,500. Thus, in period 2, the tax revenue collected is $150 \times \$1,500 = \$225,000$ and the benefit per retiree is $\$225,000/100 = \$2,250$. Each person who paid a tax of $1,000 in period 1 and receives a benefit of $2,250 in period 2 obtains a return on Social Security saving of 125% (or ($2,250/$1,000) − 1).

This can be generalized as follows. Under PAYGO, benefits paid each period equal taxes collected that period. The benefits paid are BR (where B is the benefit per retiree and R is the number of retirees), and the payroll taxes paid are twL (where t is the PAYGO wage tax rate, w is the wage per worker, and L is the number of workers). Thus, in period 2 (when the person is a retiree), $B_2 R_2 = t_2 w_2 L_2$, implying that $B_2 = t_2 w_2 L_2 / R_2$. Since the number of retirees in period 2 (R_2) equals the number of workers in period 1 (L_1), it follows that $B_2 = t_2 w_2 L_2 / L_1$. In period 1, the worker paid tax $T_1 = t_1 w_1$. Thus, the yield $\mathbf{r}$, which by definition equals $[(B_2/T_1)-1]$, equals $[(t_2 w_2 L_2 / L_1)/t_1 w_1]-1$, so $\mathbf{r} = (t_2/t_1)(w_2/w_1)(L_2/L_1) - 1$. In the steady state, $t_2 = t_1$, so $\mathbf{r} = (w_2/w_1)(L_2/L_1) - 1$. Assume the real (inflation-adjusted) wage grows at roughly the same rate as real output per worker (productivity) g, so that $(w_2/w_1) = (1+g)$, and that $L_2/L_1 = (1+n)$, where n is the growth rate of labor. Then $\mathbf{r} = n + g + ng$, the growth rate of labor plus the growth rate of productivity plus the product of the growth rates.

Output (Y) is the product of output per worker (A) and the number of workers (L), so $Y = AL$; the growth rate of output is

$$(Y_2/Y_1) - 1 = (A_2 L_2 / A_1 L_1) - 1 = (A_2/A_1)(L_2/L_1) - 1$$
$$= (1+g)(1+n) - 1 = n + g + ng.$$

Thus, the return $\mathbf{r}$ on Social Security equals the growth rate of real output. It can be shown that this result holds in a multiyear model (Seidman 1983).

APPENDIX 2B: AN EXAMPLE OF FUNDED VERSUS PAYGO SOCIAL SECURITY

Tables 2B.1 and 2B.2 give a numerical example of funded Social Security versus the PAYGO Social Security it would replace. The numbers come from a standard two-period life cycle growth model and are derived in Appendix 2C. The numbers are not intended to be empirically realistic, but they are useful in providing concreteness.

In this model, each person works in stage 1 and retires in stage 2 (the periods are of equal length). Each worker earns a wage, receives no inheritance, pays a wage (payroll) tax, saves privately, and consumes. Each retiree earns interest income (investment income), receives a Social Security benefit, withdraws private wealth accumulated from saving, and consumes (leaving no bequest). The worker's wage equals the marginal product of labor and the retiree's interest rate equals the marginal product of capital. There is no technological progress or productivity growth. Labor growth per period is 50%, so output growth per period is 50% and hence the yield on PAYGO Social Security saving is 50%. Given the Social Security system (funded or PAYGO), each person chooses a feasible consumption path for stages 1 and 2 to maximize lifetime utility.

With funded Social Security, we assume that each person has two wealth accounts (a private account A and a Social Security account F) yielding the same interest rate r, and that the person treats the two accounts as perfect substitutes. It follows that the steady-state capital per worker with funded Social Security is the same as with no Social Security. The allocation of wealth between the two accounts depends on the payroll tax rate of the Social Security fund. A higher tax rate causes more wealth to be allocated to F and therefore less to A. Thus, the right column of Table 2B.1 is identical with the left column except for two rows: with no Social Security, the payroll tax of a worker is 0.000 and private saving of a worker is 1.500; with funded Social Security, the payroll tax of a worker is 0.540 and the private saving of a worker is 0.960, so that the total saving of a worker is again 1.500.

70

Table 2B.1. *The Economy*

	No Social Security	Social Security	
		PAYGO	Funded
Capital per worker	1.000	0.533	1.000
Output per worker	6.000	5.126	6.000
Consumption per worker	5.500	4.860	5.500
Investment per worker	0.500	0.266	0.500
Investment rate of economy	8.33%	5.20%	8.33%
Wage of a worker	4.500	3.845	4.500
Consumption of a worker	3.000	2.276	3.000
Payroll tax of a worker	0.000	0.769	0.540
Private saving of a worker	1.500	0.799	0.960
Consumption of a retiree	3.750	3.875	3.750

Table 2B.1 focuses on the economy. Capital per worker is only 53.3% as large with PAYGO Social Security (0.533 vs. 1.000). For illustration, consider the funded column. Output per worker (6.000) is the sum of consumption per worker (5.500) plus investment per worker (0.500). The investment rate of the economy (8.33%) equals investment per worker divided by output per worker (8.33% = 0.500/6.000). The wage of a worker (4.500) equals the consumption of a worker (3.000) plus the payroll tax of a worker (0.540) plus the private saving of a worker (0.960). Note that consumption per worker (5.500) equals the consumption of a worker (3.000) plus the consumption of a retiree per worker (2.500, or 3.750/1.500).

Table 2B.2 focuses on Social Security. The payroll tax rate under both types of Social Security is set to achieve the same

Table 2B.2. *Social Security*

	No Social Security	Social Security	
		PAYGO	Funded
Replacement rate		30%	30%
Benefit per retiree		1.153	1.350
Capital per worker	1.000	0.533	1.000
Privately owned capital per worker	1.000	0.533	0.640
Fund capital per worker		0.000	0.360
Share of capital owned by the fund		0%	36%
Interest rate per period	150%	240.5%	150%
Yield on Social Security saving		50%	150%
Payroll tax rate		20%	12%
Wage per worker	4.500	3.845	4.500
Payroll tax per worker		0.769	0.540
Fund interest per worker		0.000	0.540
Fund inflow per period		0.769	1.080
Tax share of fund inflow		100%	50%
Investment income share of fund inflow		0%	50%
Benefit per worker		0.769	0.900
Fund surplus per worker		0.000	0.180
Benefit share of fund inflow		100%	83.3%
Surplus share of fund inflow		0%	16.7%

30% replacement rate (the benefit per retiree is lower with PAYGO, 1.153 vs. 1.350, and the wage per worker is lower, 3.845 vs. 4.500). With PAYGO, not only is capital per worker much lower (53.3% of its value with funded Social Security), but even privately owned capital is lower (0.533 vs. 0.640). With funded Social Security, 36% (0.360/1.000) of the capital stock is owned by the Social Security fund. Because capital per worker is lower with PAYGO, the interest rate (which equals the marginal product of capital) is higher (240.5% vs. 150%), but the yield on funded Social Security saving equals its interest rate of 150%, in contrast to the 50% yield with PAYGO (equal to the growth rate of labor or output).

With funded Social Security, the same replacement rate is achieved with a much lower tax rate (12% vs. 20%). Multiplying the tax rate by the wage per worker yields payroll tax per worker. This is the only component of fund inflow per worker under PAYGO (0.769), but it is one of two components with funded Social Security: payroll tax per worker (0.540) and fund interest per worker (0.540), for a total inflow of 1.080. The tax share of fund inflow is 50% and the investment income share of fund inflow is 50%. Of this fund inflow, 83.3% (0.900) is used to pay retiree benefits and the remaining 16.7% (0.180) is surplus used to buy capital so that fund capital grows 50% (0.18/0.36) per period, matching labor's growth rate of 50% and thereby keeping fund capital per worker constant at 0.36.

This example illuminates a crucial point about funded Social Security. The annual inflow that finances benefits does not come solely from investment income earned by the Social Security portfolio. With funded Social Security, an important share of the annual inflow continues to come from payroll taxes. In this example, it happens that the two shares are equal.

APPENDIX 2C: SOCIAL SECURITY IN A TWO-PERIOD
LIFE-CYCLE GROWTH MODEL

This standard two-period life-cycle growth model is used to derive the numbers presented in the two tables of Appendix 2B.

Funding Social Security

We compare three steady states: no Social Security, PAYGO Social Security, and funded Social Security.

Without Social Security

In all periods, each worker provides one unit of labor (there is no labor-augmenting technical progress). The production function is $Y = mK^\alpha L^{1-\alpha}$, where m is a constant, K is capital, L is labor, and α is a constant between 0 and 1. Hence

$$(1) \qquad y = mk^\alpha, \quad 0 < \alpha < 1,$$

where y is output per worker and k is capital per worker. There is no capital depreciation. It can be shown that the marginal product of labor (MPL) equals $(1 - \alpha)mk^\alpha$ and that the marginal product of capital (MPK) equals $\alpha m/k^{1-\alpha}$. We assume that each factor is paid its marginal product, so

$$(2) \qquad w = (1 - \alpha)mk^\alpha,$$

$$(3) \qquad r = \alpha m/k^{1-\alpha},$$

where w is the wage per worker and r is the rental per unit of capital (the interest rate). Output consists of consumption plus investment, so

$$(4) \qquad y \equiv c + i,$$

where c is consumption per worker and i is investment per worker. The number of workers grows at the rate $n > 0$. Thus, in every period v,

$$(5) \qquad L[v] = L[0](1 + n)^v,$$

so in this two-stage model, the worker/retiree ratio is $(1 + n)$. Each person works in stage 1 and retires in stage 2. The two

74

Funded versus PAYGO Social Security

stages are of equal length and each person lives two periods. Each worker supplies labor and each retiree supplies capital to a firm. Each person earns a wage w in stage 1, consumes C_1, and saves S_1; each retiree is paid interest rS_1 and consumes $C_2 = (1+r)S_1 = (1+r)(w - C_1)$, so that

$$(6) \qquad C_1 + [C_2/(1+r)] = w$$

is the lifetime budget constraint. Each individual's lifetime utility function is Cobb–Douglas, so

$$(7) \qquad U = C_1^\beta C_2^{1-\beta}, \quad 0 < \beta < 1.$$

The individual chooses the (C_1, C_2) that maximizes (7) subject to the constraint (6). Using the Lagrange multiplier method, we find that this person chooses

$$(8) \qquad C_1 = \beta w.$$

Since $S_1 = w - C_1$, the person chooses

$$(9) \qquad S_1 = (1 - \beta)w,$$
$$(10) \qquad C_2 = (1 - \beta)w(1 + r).$$

At the end of the work stage, the individual saves S_1, so the saving of a worker is $S_1[v]$ in time period v, the capital of a *retiree* in period $[v + 1]$ is $S_1[v]$, and the capital per *worker* in period $[v + 1]$ is

$$(11) \qquad k[v + 1] = S_1[v]/(1 + n).$$

Hence, by (9) and (11),

$$(12) \qquad k[v + 1] = (1 - \beta)w[v]/(1 + n).$$

We now write (2) for period v:

$$(2v) \qquad w[v] = (1 - \alpha)m(k[v])^\alpha.$$

75

The two basic equations of the model are (2v) and (12). Equation (2v) is based on profit maximization by the firm. Equation (12) is based on utility maximization by the individual. To find the steady-state capital per worker k of the model, we set $k[v + 1] = k[v] = k$ and $w[v] = w$ in (2v) and (12), where k and w are the steady-state values. Thus, we have two equations and two endogenous variables, k and w. Solving (2v) and (12), we obtain the steady-state capital per worker, k:

$$(13) \qquad k = [(1 - \alpha)m(1 - \beta)/(1 + n)]^{1/(1-\alpha)}.$$

From (13) and (3), the steady-state interest rate is

$$(14) \qquad r = \alpha(1 + n)/(1 - \alpha)(1 - \beta).$$

In the steady state, capital and labor grow at the same rate n. The growth rate of capital is i/k, where i is investment (saving) per worker, so

$$(15) \qquad i/k = n.$$

The investment (saving) rate of the economy is the endogenous variable $s \equiv i/y$. By (15) and (1),

$$(16) \qquad s = nk^{1-\alpha}/m,$$

so for $n > 0$, the steady-state s varies directly with the steady-state k. Substituting (13) into (16) yields

$$(17) \qquad s = [n/(1 + n)](1 - \alpha)(1 - \beta).$$

Total consumption per worker, c, equals worker consumption per worker, C_1, plus retiree consumption per worker, $C_2/(1+n)$, where C_2 is retiree consumption per retiree:

$$(18) \qquad c = C_1 + [C_2/(1 + n)].$$

The parameter values that generate Table 2B.1 and Table 2B.2 are $\alpha = 0.25$, $\beta = 2/3$, $n = 50\%$, and $m = 6.000$. The left columns in Table 2B.1 and Table 2B.2 are obtained as follows. From (13), capital per worker $k = 1.000$; from (1), output per worker $y = 6.000$; from (2), the wage per worker $w = 4.500$; from (3) or (14), the interest rate $r = 150\%$; from (8), the consumption of a worker $C_1 = 3.000$; from (9), the saving of a worker $S_1 = 1.500$; from (10), the consumption of a retiree $C_2 = 3.750$; from (18), consumption per worker $c = 5.500$; from (15), investment per worker $i = 0.500$. Note that (4) holds, since $5.500 + 0.500 = 6.000$. From (17), the saving (investment) rate $s = 8.33\%$. Capital grows at rate $i/k = 0.500/1.000 = 50\%$, confirming (15).

With PAYGO Social Security

In each period there is a balanced budget, so $B_p R = t_p w L$, where the subscript p indicates PAYGO; B_p is the benefit per retiree, R is the number of retirees, t_p is the PAYGO wage (payroll) tax rate, and L is the number of workers. Recall that the worker/ retiree ratio L/R equals $(1 + n)$. Thus, the replacement rate B_p/w is given by

(19P) $$B_p/w = t_p(1 + n),$$

so $B_p = t_p w(1 + n)$. Each period a worker pays a tax equal to $T_p = t_p w$ and the next period (as a retiree) receives a benefit equal to B_p. The rate of return $\mathbf{r}$ that a worker receives on her PAYGO Social Security "saving" (payroll tax) is defined as

(20P) $$\mathbf{r} \equiv (B_p/T_p) - 1.$$

Because $B_p = t_p w(1 + n)$ and $T_p = t_p w$,

(21P) $$\mathbf{r} = n.$$

Note that (21P) depends on the assumption that there is no labor-augmenting technical progress (productivity growth) in our model. Now the lifetime budget constraint is

$$C_2 = (1+r)S_1 + B_p = (1+r)[(1-t_p)w - C_1)] + B_p;$$

using (19P), it becomes

(6P) $C_1 + [C_2/(1+r)] = \{(1-t_p) + [t_p(1+n)/(1+r)]\}w.$

An individual chooses the (C_1, C_2) that maximizes (7) subject to the constraint (6P). Using the Lagrange multiplier method, we find that this person chooses β times the right side of (6P), so

(8P) $C_1 = \beta\{(1-t_p) + [t_p(1+n)/(1+r)]\}w.$

Then, since $S_1 = (1-t_p)w - C_1$,

(9P) $S_1 = \{(1-t_p)(1-\beta) - \beta t_p[(1+n)/(1+r)]\}w.$

Because $C_2 = S_1(1+r) + B_p$, using (9P) gives

(10P) $C_2 = \{(1-t_p)(1-\beta) - \beta t_p[(1+n)/(1+r)]\}$
$$\times\, w(1+r) + t_p w(1+n).$$

Combining (9P) and (11) yields

(12P) $k[v+1]$
$$= \{[(1-t_p)(1-\beta)/(1+n)] - [\beta t_p/(1+r)]\}w[v].$$

The two basic equations of the model are (2v) and (12P). Equation (2v) is based on profit maximization by the firm. Equation (12P) is based on utility maximization by the individual. Note that, in contrast to (12), equation (12P) contains r (the interest rate). Hence we now need equation (3), which, like (2), is based on profit maximization. To find the steady-state values, we set $k[v+1] = k[v] = k$ and $w[v] = w$

78

in (2v) and (12P), where k and w are the steady-state values. We have three equations and three endogenous variables (k, w, and r). Combining (2v) and (12), we obtain $k^{1-\alpha}/(1-\alpha)m = [(1-t_p)(1-\beta)/(1+n)] - [\beta t_p/(1+r)]$; using (3) to replace $k^{1-\alpha}$ by $\alpha m/r$, we obtain an equation that implicitly yields the steady-state r (note that r appears on both sides of the equation):

(13P) $r = [\alpha/(1-\alpha)]/\{[(1-t_p)(1-\beta)/(1+n)] - [\beta t_p/(1+r)]\}$.

With these parameter values ($\alpha = 0.25$, $\beta = 2/3$, $n = 50\%$, $m = 6.00$, $t_p = 20\%$), equation (13P) becomes $r = (1/3)/\{[(0.8)(1/3)/(1.5)] - [(2/3)(0.2)/(1+r)]\}$, so $0.8r^2 - 1.3r - 1.5 = 0$ and thus $r = 240.5\%$. The middle columns of Tables 2B.1 and 2B.2 are obtained as follows. From (3), capital per worker $k = 0.533$. From (1), output per worker $y = 5.126$. From (2), the wage $w = 3.845$, and the payroll tax of a worker $t_p w = 0.769$. From (8P), the consumption of a worker $C_1 = 2.276$. From (9P), the saving of a worker $S_1 = 0.799$. From (10P), the consumption of a retiree $C_2 = 3.875$. From (18), consumption per worker $c = 4.860$. From (15), investment per worker $i = 0.266$. Note that (4) holds, since $4.860 + 0.266 = 5.126$. The investment (saving) rate $s = i/y = 5.20\%$. From (19P) the replacement rate $B_p/w = 30\%$; hence, the benefit per retiree $B_p = 1.153$. From (21P), the yield **r** on Social Security saving is 50%.

With Funded Social Security

With funded Social Security, we assume that each person has two wealth accounts – a private account A and a Social Security account F – that yield the same interest rate r and that individuals treat as perfect substitutes (Kotlikoff 1996). Let S_1 be a worker's total saving in both A and F accounts. Just as with no Social Security, each retiree's consumption C_2 equals $(1+r)S_1 = (1+r)(w - C_1)$, so the budget constraint remains (6). Just as deposits into (and withdrawals from) the A account do not appear in a person's lifetime budget constraint equation, neither do deposits into and withdrawals from the F account. An individual chooses (C_1, C_2) to maximize the same utility function (7) subject to the same budget constraint (6). Hence, equations (8)–(18) are the same as with no Social Security. It follows that the steady-state k with funded Social Security is the same as with no Social Security.

The allocation of wealth between the two accounts depends on the payroll tax rate t_f of the Social Security fund. A higher t_f causes more wealth to be allocated to F and therefore less to A. Thus, the right column of Table 2B.1 is identical with the left column except for two rows: with no Social Security, the payroll tax of a worker is 0.000 and the private saving of a worker is 1.500; with funded Social Security, the payroll tax of a worker is 0.540 (explained in a moment) and the private saving of a worker is 0.960, so that the total saving of a worker is again 1.500.

In the PAYGO steady state, by (19P) the replacement rate B_p/w equals $t_p(1 + n)$. We assume that funded Social Security must maintain the same replacement rate, $t_p(1 + n)$, so the required benefit is

$$(22F) \qquad\qquad B_f = t_p(1 + n)w.$$

However, for each person, the return on Social Security saving $(t_f w)$ equals the interest rate r, so

$$(23F) \qquad\qquad B_f = (1 + r)t_f w.$$

Funded versus PAYGO Social Security

Combining (22F) and (23F) yields

(24F) $$t_f/t_p = [(1 + n)/(1 + r)].$$

With $n = 50\%$ and $r = 150\%$ we have $t_f/t_p = 60\%$, so with $t_p = 20\%$ the funded payroll tax rate $t_f = 12\%$. In Table 2B.2, the payroll tax of a worker, $t_f w$, is 0.540; since total saving (private plus payroll tax) of a worker is 1.500, private saving of a worker is 0.960. From (23F), the funded benefit per retiree is $B_f = 1.350$; hence the replacement rate, $B_f/w = 30\%$, is the same as with PAYGO Social Security.

    With funded Social Security, capital per worker k is the same as with no Social Security. A share of the capital stock is owned directly by the Social Security fund (indirectly by individuals), and the remaining share is owned directly by individuals. We next obtain Social Security fund capital per worker, k_f. The fund inflow – payroll tax revenue and fund interest income – that is *not* used to pay benefits equals the fund's surplus. Thus, $U_f \equiv t_f w + r k_f - [B_f/(1+n)]$, where U_f is the fund surplus per worker, $t_f w$ is the tax per worker, $r k_f$ is fund interest per worker, and $B_f/(1+n)$ is the benefit per worker. Recall that $t_p w_p$ is the tax per worker in the PAYGO steady state, which equals the benefit per worker in the PAYGO steady state; to maintain the PAYGO replacement rate when w is greater than w_p, the benefit per worker must be raised by the proportion w/w_p so that the benefit per worker equals $(t_p w_p)(w/w_p) = t_p w$. Thus we obtain

(25F) $$U_f = t_f w + r k_f - t_p w.$$

Since U_f is fund surplus per worker and k_f is fund capital per worker, U_f/k_f equals the ratio of fund surplus to fund capital – that is, the growth rate of fund capital. In the steady state, this growth rate must equal the growth rate n of labor, so that k_f stays constant. Hence,

(26F) $$U_f/k_f = n.$$

Combining (25F) and (26F) yields $k_f = (t_p - t_f)w/(r - n)$, so $k_f/k = (t_p - t_f)(w/k)/(r - n)$. From (2), we have $(w/k) = (1 - \alpha)mk^{\alpha-1}$; from (3), $r = \alpha mk^{\alpha-1}$, so $r(1 - \alpha)/\alpha = (1 - \alpha)mk^{\alpha-1}$. Hence, $(w/k) = r/[\alpha/(1 - \alpha)]$ and

(27F) $$k_f/k = (t_p - t_f)r/[\alpha/(1 - \alpha)](r - n).$$

With the previous parameter values, from (27F) it follows that the share of capital owned by the fund is $k_f/k = 36\%$. Since $k = 1.000$, we have $k_f = 0.360$. From (26F), fund surplus per worker $U_f = 0.180$. The growth rate of fund capital is $U_f/k_f = 50\%$. The fund inflow per worker is $t_f w + rk_f = 1.080$; both the tax share and the interest share of the inflow equal 50%. The fund benefit per worker is $B_f/(1 + n) = 0.900$. Thus, 83.33% of the fund inflow is used to pay benefits (0.900/1.080), and 16.67% of the inflow is surplus that makes fund capital grow at the same rate (50%) as labor, thereby holding k_f constant at 0.360.

3

Funded versus Privatized Social Security

Funded versus Privatized Social Security

This chapter compares funded Social Security with privatized Social Security. In this book, "privatized Social Security" means a defined-contribution plan, where retirees receive benefits that depend on the accumulation in their own personal funds and where individuals possess ownership and control of their own portfolios and have the choice of whether to purchase an annuity upon retirement.

There is important common ground shared by funded and privatized Social Security. Both are likely to raise the national saving rate and capital accumulation. Both would entail investment in the stock market. Both are likely to achieve a higher yield on average than PAYGO Social Security. This common ground is emphasized in Seidman (1998a). As Auerbach (1997) writes: "Much of the current excitement about privatization stems from a misunderstanding about what it can do. . . . It is simple economics that the same market rate of return could be delivered by a funded public system" (p. 71).

This chapter concentrates on the differences between funded and privatized Social Security.

FERRARA'S CASE FOR PRIVATIZATION

Peter Ferrara of the Cato Institute has been a leading advocate of privatized Social Security for nearly two decades (Ferrara 1982). In a recent article (1997), he sets out his case for privatization. Most of his argument, however, is a critique of PAYGO Social Security and so provides support for funded Social Security as well as privatized Social Security. However, he ignores the option of funded Social Security, so that the reader is left with the erroneous impression that there are only two options: PAYGO or privatized Social Security. Here we focus only on passages that support privatized (but not funded) Social Security.

Ferrara emphasizes that privatization would give each worker direct personal control over employee and employer contributions to Social Security each year. By controlling their own accounts and investments, individuals would be able to tailor their retirement and insurance benefits to their own specific needs and circumstances. Workers would be able to choose their own retirement age or the level of life and disability insurance.

He also emphasizes that any privatization proposal should assure current retirees that they will not be affected by the reforms. Current retirees have paid Social Security taxes all their lives, relying on the government's promise of benefits, so this promise must be kept. At this point, Ferrara does not explain that this will require current workers to contribute to their own accounts while simultaneously paying the benefits due current and future retirees under the PAYGO system. Any system that funds Social Security – whether funded Social Security or privatized Social Security – faces this transitional problem and therefore involves short-term losses to certain age cohorts during the transition.

Ferrara sets out his preferred approach to privatization. Workers would be given the option of providing for their retirement, survivors, and disability benefits through a private investment account, like an IRA (individual retirement account), rather than through Social Security. For those who choose this option, the worker and employer would each pay 5 percentage points of the current 6.2% Social Security tax into the private account. Workers would be required to purchase private life and disability insurance covering the same survivors and disability benefits as Social Security. The same rules, regulations, and restrictions would apply to the private retirement accounts as apply to IRAs today. To reduce fraud and abuse, workers would be required to choose from among approved private investment companies to manage their account investments. Companies would apply to the federal government to obtain such approval.

Benefits at retirement would equal what the accumulated funds would support; the worker could either purchase a private annuity or make regular, periodic withdrawals. Regulations would restrict withdrawals so the retiree could not exhaust funds too soon and then be left without retirement support. For workers who choose the private option, the government would pay "recognition bonds" into their accounts, compensating them for past taxes paid into the Social Security system; the amount of the bonds would be set so that, with interest, they would pay a proportion of future benefits equal to the proportion of lifetime Social Security taxes paid. At retirement, workers would cash their bonds. The government would guarantee all workers a minimum benefit that would be financed out of general revenues. Workers would be free to stay in the public Social Security system instead of taking the private account option. There would be no benefit reductions for anyone currently receiving Social Security.

Ferrara concedes that there is a transitional burden: the cost of the increased saving to achieve a fully funded system. He contends that the cost of that saving is the same as the cost of any increase in saving – foregone current consumption – and that bearing the cost is worthwhile because of the high returns earned by the increase in saving. Ferrara rejects a method that some have suggested: selling new government bonds to finance the benefits for current retirees. He does note that issuing new bonds would enable the transition to be financed over several generations instead of imposing all the cost on the first generation. However, Ferrara correctly points out that issuing new bonds would reduce the saving generated by the reform because the increase in saving resulting from contributions to the private retirement accounts each year would be offset by the government's borrowing private savings through its sale of bonds. For this reason, he concludes, it would be wise to limit such bond financing.

Ferrara, however, is averse to any increase in the tax rate. He proposes slower benefit growth, cuts in other government spending, tax revenue feedback he expects from faster economic growth, and tax revenue on the investment income of the privatized funds. It is not clear, however, that this will be sufficient. By contrast, recall from Chapter 2 that funded Social Security prescribes a combination of slower benefit growth and payroll tax increases to run larger surpluses in order to accumulate the large capital fund required by funded Social Security (with low-income households protected by the earned-income tax credit). This is the method implicit in Feldstein and Samwick's (1997) simulation paper on privatizing Social Security; it speeds the accumulation of a higher capital stock.

Recall that, in his 1975 article (passage quoted in Chapter 2), Feldstein stated that the transition would involve an initial increase in the payroll tax rate. He defended this tax increase by pointing out that Social Security taxes will eventually have to be raised owing to demographic pressures and that, by raising the taxes sooner, they can be reduced in the long run because the investment income of the Social Security fund will be available to pay part of the cost of future benefits. According to Feldstein, if we are unwilling to raise the tax rate now then we will be unfair to the next generation, because they will have to pay a much higher tax rate to support us than the rate that we charged ourselves. Moreover, if they refuse to bear a greater burden than we are willing to bear, our benefits as retirees will be much smaller than expected.

In a recent article, Martin Feldstein (1998) explains why he prefers privatized Social Security to funded Social Security (which he proposed in his 1975 article).

> As Laurence Seidman notes in his article in this issue of the *Public Interest,* I originally advocated fully funding Social Security nearly 25 years ago using a single government-managed fund rather than individual accounts. While many of the advantages of a fully funded system that I will discuss in the current paper could be achieved if the government accumulated the funds in a single national account, I believe that a system of individual accounts, similar to popular IRAs and 401(k) plans, would have substantial advantages over a single government fund. (p. 4)

Feldstein devotes a section entitled "Individual accounts or a government fund?" to this fundamental choice. He writes:

> A common feature of the "privatized" Social Security pension systems that now exists in other countries is that they permit individuals to contribute their mandatory saving to individual accounts that can be invested in private financial assets. Some proponents of replacing the

89

existing pay-as-you-go system with a funded system do not favor mandatory saving and individual accounts but advocate using a higher payroll tax rate to accumulate a larger government trust fund that would be invested in private stocks and bonds. The existing defined-benefit structure of Social Security benefits would be retained. This form of prefunding might, in principle, be able to achieve the benefits of the higher rate of return associated with increased capital formation. It could, therefore, permit funding future benefits at a much lower cost than the existing pay-as-you-go system. I nevertheless believe that the goals of reform would be much better served with mandatory contributions to individual personal retirement accounts. (p. 13)

Feldstein says there are several reasons why he favors individual accounts. First, he points out that there is a risk that building a single government fund will not raise the capital stock because it will induce offsetting government borrowing. If Social Security is included in official government budget reports and targets, then running a surplus in Social Security might simply induce Congress to run a comparable deficit in the rest of the budget. However, individual accounts would be automatically excluded from the government budget.

Second, there will be political pressures to affect the selection of corporate stocks – for example, to exclude the stock of companies that make controversial products or are located in politically controversial countries. There might be pressure to achieve a geographical balance in choosing corporate stock, just as there is with the defense budget. Such political interference would reduce the return on the portfolio.

Third, an individual account permits each household to choose among varying retirement packages that will be offered by competing private firms – for example, packages that differ in their mixture of defined-benefit and defined-contribution components. Competition should also improve the quality of service to households. A single Social Security is a monopoly that offers the same package for everyone and feels no competitive pressure to provide good service.

Fourth, if the single fund is invested conservatively in a broad market index, it might weaken the role of capital markets in allocating funds to riskier companies with higher expected returns. With individual accounts, savers who prefer such companies will be free to channel their savings into high-risk companies.

Finally, preserving a single centralized Social Security system lets politicians continue to redistribute in favor of certain groups, such as single-earner households or older workers. Individual accounts prevent such redistribution because each retiree receives whatever has accumulated from his own past contributions.

Feldstein acknowledges that a system of individual accounts faces administrative challenges. He recommends that each employer send a single check on behalf of all employees to a single financial intermediary (a bank, mutual fund, or securities firm); the intermediary would forward each employee's contribution to the particular approved investment chosen by that employee. Based on the record of mutual funds and 401(k) plans in the United States, Feldstein estimates that the annual administrative cost would be less than 1% of assets, much less than the difference between the rate of return of a funded system and a PAYGO system.

91

THE PSA PLAN OF FIVE MEMBERS OF THE ADVISORY COUNCIL ON SOCIAL SECURITY

Five members of the Advisory Council on Social Security (Bok, Combs, Schieber, Vargas, and Weaver) support privatized Social Security as the second tier of a two-tier system. The first tier would provide an equal-dollar minimum benefit for all full-career workers, and the second tier would provide fully funded and individually owned defined-contribution retirement accounts, referred to as personal security accounts (PSAs). Under their plan, 5 of the current 6.2 percentage points paid by employees would be directed into the worker's PSA. These accounts would be individually owned and privately managed, subject to regulations assuring that they were invested in financial instruments widely available in financial markets and were held for retirement purposes; PSA accounts would not be held or managed by the government. Each individual would have a large set of investment options and would not be required to buy an annuity at retirement. Individuals could begin withdrawing funds from their accounts at age 62, and any funds remaining in their accounts at death could be included in their estates.

The PSA advocates explain how current retirees and workers who have paid Social Security taxes during their work career would be taken care of, despite this redirection of 5 percentage points to the new PSA accounts: their benefits would be financed by a combination of additional taxes and borrowing. According to Social Security Administration actuaries, a 1.52% supplement to the payroll tax would cover these transition costs over the next 72 years.

Mitchell and Zeldes (1996) assess this kind of two-tier privatization plan. They conclude that the advantages of such a plan are less political risk, more household portfolio choice, and better work incentives. The disadvantages are less redistribution, less national risk sharing, and higher administrative costs.

In his book (1996), Francis Cavanaugh, the first executive director of the Federal Thrift Retirement Board (which administers the Thrift Savings Plan for federal employees), makes several comments concerning privatized Social Security. Recall from Chapter 2 that Cavanaugh once opposed investing Social Security or other government funds in the stock market because of concern about government interference with private corporations, but that he has since changed his mind owing to the availability of broad stock index funds. Cavanaugh makes the following fundamental point about privatized Social Security.

> Another defect in the privatization option is that it would foolishly shift investment risk from the group (all Social Security participants) to the individual. This violates the fundamental insurance principle of shifting risk from the individual to the group; risk is more easily borne if it is widely distributed. Also, Social Security is a social insurance system in which the government guarantees a level of benefits, and these benefits can be provided at a lower cost if the investment risk is retained by the fund rather than shifted to the individual. (pp. 103–4)

Henry Aaron of the Brookings Institution emphasizes that the crucial question is who bears the risk under privatization:

93

Investment returns may fall short of expectations. Who should bear these risks? All privatization plans put the risk on the individual. Each worker bears the full consequence of shortfalls in deposits or returns on his or her individual account, and the pension is reduced proportionally. This is an inescapable characteristic of "defined-contribution" plans in which the contribution rate is specified, but the amount contributed depends on earnings and the ultimate benefit depends on invest- ment returns. In contrast, social insurance is a "defined- benefit" plan that diffuses risks broadly among all work- ers and across generations. The benefit formula is fixed, and workers and their employers through payroll taxes or the government through other taxes must meet those commitments. The risk workers face is political: that elected officials will change benefits or taxes. (1997, p. 21)

Aaron believes that, even if a privatized defined-contribution plan offers a higher expected return, the sure bet of a government defined-benefit plan (social insurance) is preferable. He argues that a large share of households have few assets and therefore are unable to withstand financial reverses that will inevitably arise from individual investment accounts.

But Aaron does not concede that the privatized plan will have the higher expected return. He claims that if both plans invest in the same assets, the returns potentially available under social insurance are higher, not lower, than under private plans. Since privatization means that each person is free to choose among funds, and since the incomes of fund managers hinge on that choice, selling and administrative costs will be high. Under the Chilean privatized pension system, Aaron claims such costs have averaged 20% of fund incomes, about the same as for U.S. life insurance companies.

Quinn and Mitchell (1996) raise a series of questions concerning the PSA plan. Would a person ever be permitted to use the account for medical or other emergencies prior to retirement? Would a person ever be bailed out if investments did very poorly? Would the private annuity market perform adequately? Over time, would individual accounts expand at the expense of flat benefits, thereby undermining the antipoverty role of Social Security?

THE PROBLEM OF VOLUNTARY ANNUITIES

In the absence of Social Security, a worker and spouse about to retire would face the problem of estimating how long they are likely to live in order to determine the rate at which they should draw down their accumulated wealth. They may want to insure against running out of wealth by purchasing an annuity. By paying a fixed sum to the insurance company, they will be guaranteed an annual benefit for as long as they live. Current Social Security provides such an annuity – one in which the annual benefit is automatically adjusted for inflation and continues for a surviving spouse (a joint annuity).

Under the PSA plan, the choice of whether to buy an annuity is left to each individual. The six MB (maintenance of benefits) advocates on the ACSS believe this is a serious mistake. They argue that many retirees will not buy an annuity and will either run out of funds while living or die with an excess of funds. Those who want to buy an annuity face a problem. The insurers assume that a household seeking an annuity is likely to live longer than average, so the insurer must charge

95

a correspondingly higher price. But this discourages purchase except by those who believe they will live an unusually long time. So the price must be set still higher. This is the familiar process by which "adverse selection" may narrow or even eliminate a private insurance market.

Diamond (1997) contends that leaving annuitization to the individual and the private annuity market raises serious questions. What share of retirees would choose to buy an annuity? How would annuities be priced, and what types of annuities would be selected? For individuals who do not buy an annuity, how quickly would they spend out of wealth? Would a private annuities market suffer from a serious adverse selection problem? What is the quality of individual decision making about annuities? Currently, the individual annuities market in the United States is very small, so there is little experience to analyze. A Congressional Budget Office report (1998) entitled "Social Security Privatization and the Annuities Market" raises similar questions. The report concludes that, although the cost of private annuities might fall with an enlarged market resulting from privatization, the private annuity market may not work well because of adverse selection and myopic behavior.

The PSA advocates on the ACSS explain their decision to retain voluntary annuitization in this way: "In the end, we concluded that the tier-one benefit provided a significant degree of forced annuitization, and that any further requirement was unnecessary" (p. 117).

THE RISK FOR ELDERLY WIDOWS

The MB advocates are concerned about the treatment of spouses who worked in the home rather than the market place. They contend that in contrast to current Social Security, which provides additional spouse and survivor benefits, the PSA plan provides no assured benefit for a spouse or survivor; the spouse would have no right to any part of the funds in the worker's account, or even to information about the account balance. They believe this would generate distrust between spouses and create new opportunities for financial abandonment. Diamond (1997) discusses whether spouses who did not have paid employment will be sufficiently protected under the PSA plan. He supports mandatory joint-life annuitization in order to protect widows. He observes that Social Security is based on the assumption that minimum provision for retirement should be required. Workers are required to contribute, and no access to these funds is permitted until retirement. He says that it would be odd to require no restrictions after retirement.

The PSA advocates on the ACSS explain their decision as follows.

> The more typical situation for women in the future will be that of being a partner in a two-earner couple, where both spouses have had relatively full working careers. Two-earner couples will be most appropriately analyzed as two workers rather than as a worker and a nonworking spouse. The comparative analysis suggests that women would generally fare relatively well under the PSA proposal. (p. 124)

THE KOTLIKOFF–SACHS PRIVATIZATION PLAN

Laurence Kotlikoff of Boston University and Jeffrey Sachs of Harvard propose a personal security system (PSS) for Social

Security (1997). Their version of privatized Social Security is more restrictive than the PSA plan. Workers and their spouses must invest their PSS contributions in regulated, supervised, and diversified instruments. All fund managers must offer a similar diversified portfolio. Account balances cannot be withdrawn before age 65. At age 65, PSS balances are pooled with those of other cohort members, and the federal government uses the balances to buy annuities for all cohort members. Also, the federal government matches PSS contributions of low-income contributors "on a progressive basis" in order to achieve some redistribution.

Aaron (1997) comments directly on this plan. He asserts that, despite the regulations in their plan, it cannot escape the basic property of any privatization plan: If workers are free to switch accounts, then private firms will spend money to induce switches; but workers as a group cannot earn more than the economywide average return on investments, less selling and administrative costs. Yet they *can* earn the same return, without the extra costs, through funded Social Security.

Given the restrictions that Kotlikoff and Sachs accept for their privatization plan, it might be asked: Wouldn't it be simpler to adopt funded Social Security? Funded Social Security performs "progressive matching" when benefits are paid, rather than when contributions are made; it has the Social Security Administration handle the investments (through contracting with private firms), ensures that they are broadly diversified, and pools the investment risk and returns of all workers; finally, it implements universal annuitization.

There remains the basic difference between a defined-benefit and a defined-contribution plan. Even though both rely on portfolio returns, funded Social Security is committed to paying a benefit tied to the retiree's wage history by a legislated formula, whereas PSS pays whatever the portfolio earns. With funded Social Security, the Social Security Administration is directed to sell some of the portfolio to comply with the benefit formula. Of course, sustained poor portfolio earnings may eventually require a change in the benefit formula that reduces the wage replacement rate. But with funded Social Security, this is a last resort; with privatized Social Security, it is an automatic and immediate consequence of any decline in portfolio earnings.

THE PSA ADVOCATES' OPPOSITION TO FUNDED SOCIAL SECURITY

The five PSA members of the ACSS oppose funded Social Security. They summarize their objections as follows:

> First, we do not believe that it is desirable for the federal government to become a large investor in the private capital markets of this country. . . . We believe that with the accumulation of such vast equity holdings . . . the pressures to use the funds for socially or politically "desirable goals" would be tremendous, putting at risk not only workers' taxes and retirees' benefits, but also the allocation of capital in the economy. . . . One can easily imagine the political pressures that would come to bear on Congress to drop shares of certain companies from the index, perhaps tobacco companies or companies deemed to have unfavorable labor practices . . . .
>
> Second, we believe that if the government were to become a large investor in the private capital base of

our economy it would create tremendous conflicts of interest for the government in its role as fiduciary for Social Security participants, on the one hand, and regulator of business in the interest of the public welfare on the other. Consider, for example, the situation that we would be facing today if the government were the largest investor in tobacco companies . . . .

Third, we believe that the issues of corporate governance raised by this proposal are extremely important. . . . Social Security could become the largest shareholder, owning 5 to 10 percent of the stocks of virtually all of the largest companies in the United States . . . . (pp. 126–7)

These concerns have merit, but it is important to keep in mind that funded Social Security *prohibits* direct selection of particular stocks by personnel of the Social Security Administration. With funded Social Security, the Social Security Administration contracts with private investment firms under competitive bidding to manage the portfolio of the Social Security trust fund; each investment firm manages a share of the trust fund portfolio. Each investment firm manages Social Security's portfolio the way it manages the portfolio of a conservative, risk-averse private client; the investment firm handles stock voting as it does for such a private client. Although private management of the Social Security portfolio does not eliminate the problems raised by PSA advocates, it does provide a layer of political insulation that should reduce the problems.

The PSA advocates continue:

With the federal government holding trillions of dollars in private equities in the Social Security trust funds,

what would happen if there were a major drop in equity values? Could Congress stand idly by as the value
of Social Security's portfolio dropped? . . . Would it al-
ter its investment strategy mid-stream, turning a passive
into an active strategy? Would it resort to general revenue bailouts to "hold the trust funds harmless?" What
kind of pressure might Congress bring on the exchanges
and on financial regulators to slow market adjustments?
(p. 128)

Although concern about a stock market plunge has merit, it
seems odd when voiced by advocates of privatization. Worry
about the consequences of a market plunge might be expected
from advocates of PAYGO Social Security, but it is quite sur-
prising to hear from advocates of privatized Social Security.
Consider the consequences of a stock market plunge with privatized Social Security. Many retirees, dependent on their own
defined-contribution account, would suffer a sharp unexpected
cut in retirement benefits. Each retiree would be on his own.
By contrast, with funded Social Security, Congress would be
expected to meet its commitment to retirees under its defined-
benefit formula. This might require the managers to sell some
of the assets in its portfolio to meet commitments during a market drop. These actions could later be reversed when the stock
market resumes its long-term rise.

The six MB advocates on the ACSS reply to the objections
raised by the five PSA advocates. The former believe Social Security can maintain neutrality among companies and in stockholder voting. One method is to prohibit, by law, the voting of
any stocks held by Social Security. Another is to automatically
allocate Social Security's votes in the same proportion as other
stockholder votes. Another is to delegate voting to the private

firms that will manage the Social Security portfolio (as is the case with the Federal Thrift Saving Plan).

The MB advocates contend that political interference with portfolio investment is unlikely to be an important problem. They believe that, once neutrality is declared a basic principle of Social Security investing, the competitive political system will protect this principle. Any attempt by one party to undermine neutrality would be sharply criticized by the other party. With every worker and retiree having a stake in preserving neutrality, it is doubtful that a majority would dare to challenge it. They point to the experience of other Federal defined-benefit plans. In 1995, the Tennessee Valley Authority had about 40% of its $3.8 billion in assets invested in stocks; the Federal Reserve System had about two thirds of its $2.9 billion in assets in stocks; and the systems covering the Army–Air Force exchanges had about 80% of their $1.9 billion in assets in stocks. The MB proponents state that none of these federal systems has been politically influenced in selecting investments; nor has the Federal Retirement Thrift Board, which has been authorized since 1986 to make indexed stock investments. They continue:

> Investment of part of Social Security's accumulated funds in the stock market has the great advantage of leaving the essential principles of the system undisturbed while restoring long-term balance and offering Social Security participants the same stock investment benefits that are enjoyed by participants in other large retirement plans – state, local, and private. The investment risk is kept manageable and affordable by investing as a group rather than as individuals, and the administrative costs are, of course, very low in comparison to buying stocks and mutual funds retail and managing

millions of relatively small individual accounts (not to mention regulating these accounts and reporting them to the Internal Revenue Service). And any lingering concerns about what might go wrong with a centrally managed fund should be balanced against considerations of what might go wrong in a system such as the PSA plan requiring more than 127 million compulsory individual savings accounts . . . .

Risk for individuals investing on their own is quite a different matter from the shared risk of investing through the Social Security system or indeed via any other pension system. We do not believe the nation's basic retirement system should require everyone to bear investment risk as isolated individuals, as would be the case with a system of compulsory savings plans. A central fund broadly indexed to the stock market and investing regularly in good times and bad is at far less risk. With Social Security's investments tied to the performance of the entire U.S. economy, there would be ups and downs in returns but only very long-range trends would matter. And the assumed rate of return, while important, would be secondary to the fact that benefits would remain defined by law rather than by the relative uncertainty of individual investment decisions. (pp. 84–6)

THE WORLD BANK REPORT

In its report entitled *Averting the Old Age Crisis* (1994), a World Bank policy research team led by Estelle James recommends a "multi-pillar system," with one pillar consisting of privatized individual accounts. The recommendation is similar to the proposal of the five members of the Advisory Council who favor a two-tiered system, with one tier consisting of privatized individual accounts (PSAs). The report argues that a single public pension plan cannot handle the multiple goals of redistribution, saving, and insurance. The first pillar, like the first PSA tier, would assure a minimum income for the elderly through government PAYGO taxes and transfers. The second pillar would be fully funded to promote national saving. Thus, the report rejects PAYGO financing of the whole system. But what about the crucial choice between funded Social Security and privatized Social Security?

In its overview, the report states that publicly managed funded schemes ("provident funds") have often been unsatisfactory. These funds are often required to invest in low-yield government securities or the securities of state enterprises or public housing authorities. In its chapter on personal savings plans, the report directly addresses the choice between centralized and decentralized management. It states that centralized provident funds are run by an agent of the national government. It emphasizes that centralized provident funds are compulsory monopolies, so managers have little incentive to operate efficiently and are vulnerable to political pressures concerning investment choices. However, it notes that a centralized fund benefits from economies of scale that minimize operating costs and also that Malaysia and Singapore are examples of national provident funds with low costs and stable (though modest) returns.

The authors of the report, like other advocates of a privatized pillar, make positive reference to Chile. Even some opponents of privatization for the United States concede that it has "worked" in Chile. It is often not recognized that the Chilean system has not really existed long enough to have been fully tested. It began in the early 1980s, and because it is based on individual defined-contribution accounts, most workers who have been contributing have not yet become retirees.

An article by reporter Jonathan Friedland in the *Wall Street Journal* (1997) should remind us that the Chilean experience is still evolving. Friedland reports witnessing this scene in Santiago: as workers came off their shift at a particular factory, they were surrounded by pension-fund salespersons competing for their signatures, trying to get them to switch pension funds. According to Friedland, Chile's private pension system is now experiencing falling yields, rising costs, and "a burst of unethical practices." He reports that the number of salespeople jumped from 3,500 in 1990 to 20,000 in 1996, and the number of workers switching funds escalated from 300,000 in 1990 to 2,000,000 in 1996.

Peter Diamond (1996b) has also analyzed the Chilean system. He finds strengths as well as weaknesses, but he emphasizes its high administrative cost:

> We have come to think of privatization as a route to greater efficiency and lower costs. Thus, perhaps the most surprising aspect of the Chilean reform is the high cost of running a privatized Social Security system. Possibly, this high cost should not have been surprising, for in his 1942 classic, *Social Insurance and Allied Services,* Beveridge referred to a "markedly lower cost of administration in most forms of State Insurance." (p. 76)

Diamond says that the administrative costs of the new system include both those of the firms that manage mandatory pension funds and those of the insurance companies that produce disability insurance, life insurance, and annuities. He estimates that the average administrative cost is nearly 3% of taxable earnings, or over 20% of the roughly 13.5% of earnings paid for the program. Diamond says this cost per person is close to the cost observed in other privately managed pension systems, such as defined-benefit private pensions in the United States; however, he estimates it is roughly five times greater than the administrative costs in well-run unified government-managed systems such as the U.S. Social Security system. He finds an even greater disparity by comparing individually oriented plans in the United States to Social Security. He says the U.S. life insurance industry reports operating expenses exceeding 10% of revenues, whereas the Social Security Administration reports administrative costs that are less than 1% of revenues.

Diamond believes there are several reasons why administrative cost is much lower for a compulsory government system. First, a single compulsory system without choice possesses economies of scale. Second, such a system avoids the costs generated by competitive attempts to attract more customers. He notes that in Chile there were nearly 3.5 salespeople per 1,000 contributors, whereas total U.S. Social Security employment is only 0.5 employees per 1,000 insured workers. He concedes that costs of competition are present in many products for which the benefits of competition outweigh these costs, but he contends that the benefits of competition may be small for old-age insurance.

Diamond (1997) states that the administrative costs of individual accounts with the IRA model (such as the PSA plan) would be considerably higher than with unified government managment. He says the ACSS estimated the administrative costs to be only 0.5 basis points for a central trust fund, compared with

106

100 basis points for the PSA plan. Diamond believes the disparity would turn out to be even greater. He criticizes the Advisory Council for assuming that the ratio of administrative costs to assets would be the same for all households regardless of the level of income and assets; he contends that the ratio should be higher for low-income households because a large part of the cost is fixed per account. This is the case for record keeping and communication with account holders. Thus one should expect that, as in Chile, charges would be higher relative to assets for low earners than for high earners. Currently, many mutual funds have minimum size accounts, a rule that keeps out small accounts. Also, some mutual funds have higher charges for small accounts (by waiving some of the fees for larger accounts). Thus, when privatized Social Security brings in primarily investors with small accounts, the administrative cost per account should rise.

Diamond notes that there are other administrative costs in a privatized system. An administrative structure would be required to transfer withheld funds from employers (and the self-employed) to the financial intermediaries. This might be easy for the minority of the population currently in 401(k) plans, but it would be costly to extend this service to the majority of the population. Moreover, the rules for mandated savings are likely to differ from those of 401(k)s with respect to worker choice. It would entail considerably more administrative costs than currently, where individual records need only be adjusted on an annual basis. Currently the task of making sure that withheld taxes reach the Social Security trust funds and that individual taxable earnings are correctly recorded is handled by the IRS and the Social Security Administration (SSA). But privatization would require either the IRS or the SSA to check the destination of withheld taxes: numerous investment firms.

Funding Social Security

WOULD PRIVATIZATION EVENTUALLY LEAD TO
THE TERMINATION OF SOCIAL SECURITY?

Some would go further than privatizing Social Security. One who would do so is Milton Friedman, Nobel prizewinner in economics. He and his wife Rose Friedman propose the gradual termination of Social Security in their book *Free to Choose* (1980). They offer a two-part program for "dismantling the welfare state." The first is to reform the present welfare system by replacing numerous programs with a single comprehensive program of cash income supplements (a "negative income tax"). The second is to gradually phase out Social Security while meeting present commitments so that individuals will eventually become fully responsible for their own retirement.

To phase out Social Security, they propose the following: (1) immediately terminate the payroll tax; (2) pay retirees what they are entitled to under current law; (3) give workers a rebate of the payroll taxes they have paid; and (4) finance payments to retirees and rebates to workers by cutting government spending, raising borrowing, and raising taxes.

In contrast to the Friedmans, advocates of privatization would require individuals to save for retirement in private accounts. Nevertheless, citizens who strongly favor universal compulsory Social Security worry about whether privatization will lead to termination. Anyone who owns and controls a defined-contribution retirement fund is bound to ask whether this fund can be used for a medical emergency or for a worthy purpose such as financing college or a first home. Perhaps the answer will be "no," but advocates of compulsory Social Security believe it will be politically difficult to stick to "no." But if the fund can be used for worthy purposes, there is no guarantee that

108

enough will be saved for retirement. The Friedmans argue that individuals should be treated as responsible adults and should be "free to choose" how much to save and how much to consume. Cash welfare (a negative income tax) would prevent starvation in old age, just as it does at any other age.

Most privatization advocates argue that the government should not compel annuitization – retirees should be free to use their wealth as they see fit. The Friedmans go further and ask why the government should prohibit a younger individual from choosing to finance medical care, buy a home, or pay for college tuition instead of saving for retirement. They contend that the government should provide cash welfare for the needy of any age, and then leave individuals free to choose how much to save for retirement

Opponents of privatization worry that privatization will eventually lead to the replacement of Social Security by welfare. In fact, the Friedmans support privatization as a strategic step toward termination. Opponents of privatization fear that the Friedmans' strategy may eventually succeed.

DISTORTION OF LABOR SUPPLY

Martin Feldstein (1996) analyzes the labor supply distortion generated by the current Social Security system. Feldstein explains that privatization of Social Security would greatly reduce this distortion. If each individual has her own defined-contribution account and receives retirement benefits financed by accumulations in that account, then contributions to the account do not distort labor market behavior any more than the individual's private saving, provided the required contribution does not exceed the amount the individual would choose to save voluntarily. Distortion will remain only for individuals who would have saved less than Social Security requires.

By contrast, suppose a worker assumes that, under the current Social Security program, his future retirement benefit is largely independent of the amount of payroll tax he pays. This is not generally correct because current Social Security is only partially redistributive, so that a worker's future benefit usually does increase with the tax he pays. But it is possible that many workers ignore this partial link. If so, the tax drives a 12.4% wedge between the worker's marginal product of labor and his after-tax compensation. If there were no other tax wedge, a worker who generates $100 of product would base his labor–leisure choice on the $87.60 he keeps after tax rather than the $100 of product. Feldstein points out that this wedge comes on top of the substantial wedge already created by income taxes. If the federal rate is 28% and the state rate is 5%, the 12.4% payroll tax raises the wedge from 33% to 45.4%. Hence, a worker who generates $100 of product would base his labor–leisure choice on the $54.60 he keeps after taxes.

The magnitude of the welfare loss from this substantial tax wedge depends on the compensated "elasticity" of labor supply (the responsiveness of labor supply to the after-tax wage). Most econometric studies report a low elasticity for heads of households but a high elasticity for second earners. Feldstein (1996) argues that many of these studies underestimate the elasticity because they define labor supply too narrowly – by hours of work – and ignore other dimensions of labor supply, such as intensity of effort. The high elasticity for second earners is of particular concern because it is likely that many second earners regard their retirement benefit as independent of the payroll tax they pay, since Social Security provides a benefit to spouses who did not work in the marketplace.

Whatever the magnitude of the welfare loss from labor supply distortion, a key question is how much of the payroll tax loss would be eliminated by converting to funded Social Security instead of privatized Social Security. The answer is that a large share of the loss would be eliminated because, in the long run, the payroll tax rate required to achieve the current replacement rate (benefit/wage ratio) would be much lower than 12.4%. For example, Feldstein and Samwick (1997) estimate 2%; Seidman and Lewis (1998), 4%.

The distortion that remains from the permanent low tax rate does depend on whether it finances privatized Social Security or funded Social Security. As explained earlier, with privatized Social Security there would be no distortion from the tax rate provided each individual would have voluntarily saved as much as privatized Social Security mandates. With funded Social Security, which preserves partial redistribution from high-wage to low-wage workers, an important share of the tax would cause a distortion. This distortion is the inevitable consequence of the social insurance principle of implementing partial redistribution. In his comment on Diamond's 1997 article, Auerbach (1997) writes:

> Another alleged advantage of a private Social Security system is that it permits greater linkage between contributions and benefits, thereby reducing the taxes on labor supply implicit in the present system. Diamond points out, however, that the incomplete linkage and associated distortions in the current public system are inherent in any system that seeks to redistribute. (pp. 71–2)

CAN WORKERS MANAGE THEIR OWN
INDIVIDUAL ACCOUNTS?

The five PSA members of the ACSS believe workers can manage their own accounts. They write that critics often claim that many people are uninformed about personal investing and that the PSA plan is therefore either impractical or requires a guarantee that would ensure workers a minimum return. They reply that great improvements have been made in recent years in financial markets and in individuals' participation in them. Through the introduction of IRAs, 401(k) plans, and other similar investment vehicles, many workers and retirees have acquired experience with personal investing. Moreover, thanks to mutual funds and especially equity index funds, people need not bear large transaction costs and risk in order to participate in the stock market. Because of the competition among investment firms for individual customers, information has become widespread about investment strategies and performance. The PSA advocates believe the main reason that some people remain uninformed about personal investment is that they never have any money to invest and therefore lack the incentive to learn about investing. For the first time, the PSA plan would give such individuals an incentive to learn or to seek investment counseling.

The PSA proponents assert that people would learn quickly because they would make frequent decisions and receive frequent reports on their portfolios. Hence, learning would be easier than it is in the case of other major investment decisions, which are made very infrequently. For example, a typical household buys a new home perhaps once or twice in a lifetime. The same is true for major surgery, which may involve an element of urgency that prevents the acquisition of good information. By contrast, with PSAs, market returns would provide steady information on investment performance, and the relative success of competing financial institutions would provide valuable information. PSA advocates assert that they were presented with no convincing evidence that workers could not, with experience, make good financial decisions.

But many critics point to the low level of general education of a large segment of the adult population, and they argue that the burden of proof rests with privatization advocates who claim that the general public can master the basics of finance and investing. Moreover, critics worry that aggressive advertising by competing investment firms will generate as much misinformation as accurate information, making it harder, not easier, for the typical individual to figure out what to do.

The PSA advocates admit that not everyone will learn to be a good investor. They acknowledge that some workers will take on too little risk, others, too much. They then make an interesting statement: "We were in general agreement, however, that workers would fare better, ex ante, under this option than under the present inadequately financed system, or either of the other two options developed by the Advisory Council" (ACSS 1997, p. 115).

"Ex ante" means that, prior to investing, the expected return of the average worker would be higher with privatized Social Security than with PAYGO Social Security. But the main concern of many critics is that with privatized Social Security there will be significant variation in the ex post returns actually received by individual workers. These critics might agree with the claim about ex ante returns and nevertheless reject privatization precisely because their main concern is about the likely wide variation in ex post returns.

113

The PSA advocates oppose substantial regulation of PSA accounts. They accept the requirement that personal accounts be invested in regulated financial instruments that are widely available in financial markets, and they accept limited restrictions placed on certain categories of investments that would not be permitted in the early years of the PSA program (while the general public becomes more educated). However, they oppose regulations that would limit the freedom of workers to invest in financial instruments that are widely available today; they want workers to have the same range of options now available though 401(k) plans. They argue that worries about uninformed investors should be addressed by an educational effort, not by substantially limiting individual investment choices or by substituting government decisions for individual decisions.

Supporters of PSAs are correct in assuming that an individual household can limit its risk while probably obtaining a reasonable return if it chooses a broadly diversified index fund. But will most households in fact choose such a fund? Today, some households prefer risky undiversified portfolios concentrated on their favorite stocks, while others settle for a low return by sticking with low-risk government bonds.

The PSA advocates admit that their plan would not provide a guarantee of a reasonable return for each individual. But they argue that neither does the current system provide such a guarantee. They assert that, with the current PAYGO system, many middle-aged and younger workers are projected to earn negative rates of return on their Social Security taxes. Moreover, there is the political risk that benefits might be cut, that the cost-of-living adjustment might be reduced, and that benefits may be taxed more heavily or even means-tested. They contend that individual accounts with minimal government regulation are the best protection against political risks that, in their view, will become much larger than financial risks in the coming decades.

The PSA proponents emphasize that their proposal contains two tiers, not one. They estimate that half of Social Security financing would still utilize the traditional PAYGO defined benefit system. They explain that their first tier implements more redistribution than the current system: two workers with the same years of work but different wages will pay different dollar taxes but receive the same dollar benefits. They note that their plan's redistribution, in contrast to the current system's, is not implemented by a complex benefit formula but instead is easily grasped: the same dollar benefit for all full-career workers, prorated only for years of work. This benefit is fully cost-of-living adjusted. Their first tier is intended to ensure that, together with second-tier accumulations, all full-career workers can expect to receive a minimally adequate retirement income from Social Security, without resorting to means-tested poverty assistance.

The PSA advocates are right to emphasize the assistance that will come from the flat-benefit tier – if it is maintained at the level they recommend. But they ignore a major worry of their critics: the political risk that the flat benefit will gradually be reduced. The extreme redistribution of their first tier is obvious to the public: an equal dollar benefit for all workers with the same years of work, regardless of the worker's dollar earnings or dollar taxes paid. Since their flat benefit is much more redistributive than current Social Security, workers with above-average earnings would be much better off without the flat-benefit tier. Consequently, there is a serious political risk that the flat benefit will gradually be cut because it is viewed as welfare.

Diamond (1997) questions whether many households are prepared to choose an investment portfolio. He points out that much of the public has little or no experience choosing a portfolio. Those who save generally choose interest-bearing assets, not stocks. He says one can only guess about what those who currently do not save would do under privatized Social Security. After all, they would on average have less general education than current investors. He cites some recent evidence:

> In a telephone survey of investors, when asked, "From what you know, when interest rates go up, what usually happens to the prices of bonds? Do bond prices usually go up, go down, or do they stay about the same?", only 39% answered that bond prices go down (24% thought they go up, 19% thought they stay the same, while 18% did not know). When asked, "As far as you know, when an investor diversifies his investments, does his risk of losing money increase or decrease?", only 51% answered decrease (28% answered increase, 20% did not know, and 1% volunteered neither or stays the same) (Princeton Survey Research Associates, 1996). (p. 45)

Diamond is also concerned about fraud. Fraud is a problem even with relatively educated investors. What will happen with a large influx of inexperienced investors? How will it affect the political stability of a privatized proposal? Diamond cites the U.K. experience, with its voluntary opt-out of the earnings-related portion of their retirement income scheme. He says that its first decade has witnessed numerous complaints and lawsuits. Efforts to contain the problem include calls for overhauling the system and restricting the range of individual choice. He reports that a striking feature of the U.K. market for individual opt-out accounts is the complexity of the arrangements offered in the market. Thus, an unregulated market has the virtue of tailoring packages to heterogeneous tastes – but also the vice of confusing and taking advantage of consumers.

Diamond contends that, under a system of individual accounts, pressure for government regulation is likely to evolve in response to cases of fraud and poor investment choices. He points out that stricter regulation reintroduces the concerns about direct government control of portfolios. In a regulatory environment, pressures might develop to require prior approval of an individual's portfolio choice. Individual accounts with regulation might end up with large administrative and monitoring costs. Diamond notes that individual portfolio choice raises the question of who will control and pay for investment education of workers who must make choices. It also raises the question of whether the government will ever bail out individuals with bad portfolio outcomes. If so, by what criteria?

NINE BASIC PRINCIPLES FOR SOCIAL SECURITY

The six MB members of the ACSS who oppose individual accounts list nine principles that they regard as basic for Social Security; these principles are also delineated in Ball (1978) and in Ball and Bethell (1997): "Social Security is *universal; an earned right; wage-related; contributory and self-financed; redistributive; not means-tested; wage-indexed; inflation-protected; and compulsory*" (ACSS 1997, pp. 94–5).

The nine principles are largely met by the current U.S. PAYGO Social Security. Because funded Social Security differs from the current U.S. PAYGO system solely in its capital fund accumulation and investment portfolio, it also adheres to these

117

nine principles. Advocates of privatized Social Security do not accept four of these principles: *an earned right; wage-related; redistributive;* and *inflation-protected.*

> *Earned right:* Social Security is more than a statutory right; it is an *earned* right, with eligibility for benefits and the benefit rate based on an individual's past earnings. This principle sharply distinguishes Social Security from welfare and links it, appropriately, to other earned rights such as wages, fringe benefits, and private pensions . . . .
>
> *Wage-related:* Social Security benefits are related to earnings, thereby reinforcing the concept of benefits as an earned right and recognizing that there is a relationship between one's standard of living while working and the benefit level needed to achieve income security in retirement. Under Social Security, higher-paid earners get higher benefits – while, at the same time, the lower-paid get more for what they pay in. (p. 95)

Privatized Social Security does not accept a right to benefits based on labor earnings. With privatized Social Security, you get whatever you have accumulated in your fund, regardless of your earnings. Even if you have consistently earned an average salary during your work career, if your portfolio plunges in value at retirement then you receive a small benefit.

> *Redistributive:* One of Social Security's most important objectives is to pay at least a minimally adequate benefit to workers who are regularly covered and contributing, regardless of how low-paid they may be. This is accomplished through a redistributional formula that

pays comparatively higher benefits to low-paid than to high-paid earners. The formula and the idea behind it make good sense. If the system paid back to low-wage workers only the benefit that they could reasonably be expected to pay for on their own, millions of retirees would end up on welfare even though they had been paying into Social Security throughout their working lives. This would make the years of contributing to Social Security worse than pointless, since the earnings deductions would have reduced their income throughout their working years without providing in retirement any income above what would be available from a welfare payment. The redistributional formula solves this dilemma, and, in doing so, reduces the burden of welfare for everyone: those who would otherwise end up on it and the rest who must pay for it. (p. 95)

This principle of partial redistribution is rejected by most advocates of privatized Social Security, who believe that a central virtue of privatization is that each household receives exactly the retirement portfolio that it has accumulated over its work life. A few advocates of privatization support limited redistribution to low-income workers, not through a defined benefit formula but through federal matching of individual contributions. Feldstein and Samwick (1997), Kotlikoff and Sachs (1997), and Kotlikoff, Smetters, and Walliser (1998) all consider the possibility of limited progressive matching of individual contributions by the federal government. They do not, however, assess the prospects for politically achieving such matching – matching that is opposed by many supporters of privatization.

Another approach to partial redistribution with privatization is to have two tiers. Recall that the first tier of the PSA plan is actually more redistributive than current Social Security, while the second tier is privatized. Under the first tier, retirees with the same years of work, regardless of earnings and payroll taxes, would receive the same dollar benefit. The PSA plan clearly separates the highly redistributive first tier from the nonredistributive second tier. Yet this may cause many of the affluent to politically favor expansion of the nonredistributive second tier and contraction of the highly redistributive first tier. The current U.S. defined-benefit Social Security program has achieved political support for a benefit formula that implements partial redistribution from high-wage to low-wage workers. Splitting the program into two distinct tiers – one highly redistributive and one not redistributive at all – may weaken broad political support for the redistributive component.

> *Inflation-protected:* Once they begin, Social Security benefits are protected against inflation by periodic Cost of Living Adjustments (COLAs) linked to the consumer price index. Inflation protection is one of Social Security's great strengths, and one that distinguishes it from other (except federal) retirement plans: no private pension plan provides guaranteed protection against inflation, and inflation protection under state and local plans, where it exists at all, is capped. Without COLAs, the real value of Social Security benefits would steadily erode over time, as is the case with unadjusted private pension benefits. Although adjustment was not included in the original legislation, the importance of protecting benefits against inflation was well understood, and over the years the system was financed to allow for periodic legislation to bring benefits up to date. (ACSS 1997, p. 96)

Funded versus Privatized Social Security

Privatized Social Security does not provide direct inflation protection. If the worker purchases an annuity upon retirement, there is usually no annual adjustment for inflation. For retirees who maintain their portfolios, the nominal portfolio value may rise with inflation, thereby enabling nominal withdrawals (benefits) to rise. But there is no assurance that the retiree will be protected against inflation.

Privatized Social Security is based on the philosophy that each individual should provide individually for her own retirement. In contrast, funded Social Security is based on the philosophy set forth by the six MB members of the Advisory Council:

Social Security is a blend of reward for individual effort and, at the same time, perhaps our strongest expression of community solidarity. Social Security is based on the premise that *we're all in this together,* with everyone sharing responsibility not only for contributing to their own and their family's security but also to the security of everyone else, present and future.

There is nothing sentimental about this approach; it is neither liberal nor conservative; it simply makes sense. Unable to know in advance who will succeed and who will struggle unsuccessfully, who will suffer early death or disability and who will live long into retirement, in good health or ill, we pool our resources and are thereby able to protect against the average risk, at manageable cost to each of us. Social Security's redistributive benefits formula, feasible only in a system in which nearly everyone participates, not only helps to protect us all against impoverishment but, because it is part of a universal system, does so at much lower administrative

121

cost than private insurance and without the stigma of a welfare program. (p. 89)

Funded Social Security is a politically strategic alternative. Its strategic premise is that the best way to protect the nine principles is to make sure that a unified defined-benefit Social Security offers most workers as good a deal as low-risk private saving. This can be accomplished by gradually accumulating a large capital fund, thereby converting PAYGO Social Security to funded Social Security.

4

Funded versus PAYGO Social Security with Individual Accounts

Funded versus PAYGO with Individual Accounts

There are two middle positions between PAYGO Social Security and privatized Social Security. One is funded Social Security. The other is PAYGO Social Security with supplemental individual defined-contribution accounts. This chapter compares the two alternative middle positions.

PUBLICLY HELD INDIVIDUAL ACCOUNTS

The chairman (Gramlich, professor of economics at the University of Michigan) and one other member (Twinney) of the Advisory Council on Social Security propose supplemental individual accounts (IAs). They emphasize that such accounts are supplemental – Gramlich and Twinney favor preserving the PAYGO defined-benefit plan (with several changes to improve it). They also emphasize that there would be important restrictions concerning these individual accounts and entitle their proposal "Publicly Held Individual Accounts." Under their IA proposal, there would be a compulsory additional contribution of 1.6% of covered payroll that would be held by the government as defined-contribution individual accounts. Individuals would select from a limited menu of investment choices provided by the government (one might be bond index funds; another, equity index funds). The individual accounts would be converted by the government to inflation-protected annuities when individuals retire.

Elsewhere, Gramlich (1996) explains that the IA plan is similar to one offered in 1995 by Senators Kerrey and Simpson in that both plans would finance new individual accounts with 1.6% of payroll. However, there is a crucial difference. The Kerrey–Simpson plan would keep the total payroll tax at 12.4%, whereas the IA plan would raise it to 14%. Thus, the IA proposal roughly maintains the benefits of current retirees, because 12.4% continues to go to the PAYGO system; the 1.6% is truly supplemental.

The IA members argue that this difference is the key to raising national saving, which they regard as a high priority. The tax increase from 12.4% to 14% would be channeled into new saving through the individual accounts. They assert that there must be some new saving to finance the nation's retirement system in the coming decades.

The Kerrey–Simpson plan, like other recent proposals that will be reviewed later in this chapter, takes the contributions of individual accounts out of the existing 12.4% payroll tax. This immediately raises the question: With less than 12.4% going into the PAYGO system, how will benefits be maintained for current retirees? We will return to this crucial point shortly.

Funded Social Security, however, also prescribes a tax increase (and slowdown in benefit growth) in order to generate new saving. Funded Social Security seeks to accumulate a single large fund, whereas the IA plan seeks to accumulate many small funds. Advocates of individual accounts believe that politically it will be less difficult to achieve a tax increase earmarked for individual accounts than a tax increase earmarked for the aggregate Social Security fund. Diamond (1997), however, argues that it is not obvious which approach to raising national saving is more likely to succeed politically. He writes:

Proponents of individual accounts, wanting more fund accumulation than would occur without an immediate tax increase, argue that individual accounts would make a tax increase more likely. . . . To assess the strength of this as a political argument, one needs to consider both the popularity of Social Security (which makes an earmarked tax increase more likely than tax increases are generally) and the risk of delaying legislation as a consequence of trying simultaneously to raise taxes and to make a major change in the structure of the system . . . . (p. 39)

This point about delay deserves emphasis. With the IA plan, the earmarked tax increase can be implemented only after all the practical problems of establishing new individual accounts have been overcome. By contrast, with funded Social Security, the earmarked tax increase can be implemented prior to adopting the rules for contracting out the management of the portfolio to private firms. The tax increase that resulted from the 1983 Social Security reforms has been invested in special government bonds. This can immediately be increased in magnitude without waiting for the adoption of portfolio management rules.

Advocates of the IA approach assume that the average citizen will support a tax increase earmarked for her own individual account but not for a general Social Security account. Yet this assumption may not hold if the average citizen believes that pooling the risk is a sounder approach than individualizing the risk. The willingness of citizens to support the significant payroll tax increases of the 1980s remains a puzzle to many analysts. One possible explanation is that the average citizen regards the current defined-benefit Social Security program, where risk is pooled, as a program worth supporting even with tax increases. If citizens regard new individual accounts as a risky and untested approach, then they may prove less willing to support a tax increase to finance it.

127

The IA members emphasize that their supplemental individual accounts plan differs significantly from privatization in general and from the PSA plan in particular. They write:

> *The IA plan provides for adequate basic Social Security benefits underneath the individual accounts.* To illustrate some of the risks in the PSA plan, . . . the central flat benefit paid by the OASDI Trust Fund would be at about the poverty line. . . . Most workers will invest their PSAs well and have a decent retirement income, but some may not, and they may be forced down to this low base level standard of living. Most workers will retire when the stock market is performing normally and will not be at the mercy of a sharp decline in stock values, but some may not and may be forced down to a lower standard of living. Most disabled workers may become disabled near the end of their career and have accumulated PSAs to draw on, but some may not and be forced down to a lower standard of living.
>
> *The IA plan imposes prudent restrictions on the management of the individual accounts.* Switching to a greater public reliance on defined contribution pension accounts does introduce some new risks. . . . The IA plan deals with these risks by constricting individuals' portfolio selection to government-managed index funds. For the PSA plan, by contrast, it is very hard to see how the private PSA accounts can be effectively regulated. Many of these PSA accounts will be small, and will be held in a disparate set of financial institutions. As with IRAs, there are also political risks that Congress will permit the privately held PSAs to be used for nonretirement needs, hence defeating the purpose of

128

stimulating retirement saving, and letting another set of people arrive at their retirement age with only the low flat benefit.

The IA plan keeps fund administrative costs low. Since all the money for the individual accounts will be collected by the government and allocated to peoples' individual accounts in a way that these individuals have designated, the money does not have to be managed account by account. Allocations to separate funds can be aggregated and large checks can be sent to the money managers. For the PSA plan, by contrast, these individual accounts will have to be managed account-by-account, providing for excessive record-keeping costs for very small accounts. While some large funds may take advantage of economies of scale in managing assets, others may not. There could also be large private advertising expenses.

The IA plan requires annuitization of the accounts. . . . The IA plan simply converts fund accumulations to an annuity on retirement, and maintains the real value of this annuity under inflation, just like present Social Security benefits. As it is presently written, the PSA plan permits workers attaining age 62 full access to their accounts that have been accumulated over an entire working career. The government is in effect saying to people that it does not trust them to save for the future when they are younger than 62, so it requires them to hold PSAs. But once these people become 62 they suddenly become wise and responsible, and the government no longer requires them to preserve their assets beyond that date. This segmentation seems strange. (ACSS 1997, pp. 156–7)

The IA members also explain how their plan differs from both the MB plan and from funded Social Security. They write:

> *The IA plan gives people an explicit stake in Social Security.* The Council has heard over and over how people, especially younger people, do not trust Social Security, do not think any money will be there for them. Small-scale individual accounts will not totally change this view, but they should change it in a positive direction. With the IA plan all workers will have and manage their own accounts, and these pre-funded accounts will be protected from many of the political, economic, and demographic uncertainties facing the OASDI system. . . . Under the massive central government stock purchases of the MB plan . . . there could be any number of new difficulties. If particular firms are felt to be in violation of some ethical norm, some foreign policy principle, some labor standard, or even some political standard, there could be calls to dump the OASDI stock holdings of these firms. (p. 155)

Elsewhere, Gramlich (1996) amplifies this argument.

> One advantage of these individual accounts is that they decentralize decisions over how the funds are invested; because individuals choose how their funds will be invested, no longer is one overall board allocating the equivalent of a trillion dollars of common stock. If stocks do not perform up to expectations, individuals can blame their own investment choices and alter those choices. (p. 60)

CRITICISMS OF THE INDIVIDUAL ACCOUNTS PLAN

The six MB (maintenance of benefits) members of the ACSS fear that any introduction of individual defined contribution accounts – even the limited publicly regulated accounts proposed by the two IA members – would be the first step in the erosion of a key feature of Social Security: partial redistribution. The six MB members write:

> *The Seeds of Dissolution.* There would be every reason for many average and above-average earners, particularly, to press for further reductions in contributions to Social Security in order to make more available for their individual accounts. Thus, the IA plan is inherently unstable, and could lead to the unraveling of the redistributional provisions that are so integral to Social Security and so crucial to its effectiveness. (p. 62)

Diamond (1997) shares their concern:

> The current structure of Social Security has been politically stable. . . . Would a program that combined defined-contribution and defined-benefit elements be similarly stable? A number of arguments suggest that the IA proposal would not. . . . To the extent that individuals perceive the defined-contribution component as superior, they will generate political pressure to expand that portion and shrink the defined-benefit portion of Social Security. This may have large implications for the redistribution that happens through the system. (pp. 39–40)

The six MB members write:

Increased Risk for the Individual Family. The IA plan shifts Social Security away from being a defined-*benefit* plan and toward becoming a defined-*contribution* plan. This is a bad idea. As previously noted, Social Security is the foundation of our national multi-tier retirement system, with private pension plans and private savings built on top. With more and more private-sector employers offering only defined-contribution pension plans, it is all the more important that the nation's *basic* plan be maintained as a defined-benefit system, with the amounts available in retirement determined by law rather than by the risks and relative uncertainties of individual investment. With the basic plan secure, some level of risk in defined-contribution pension plans and investment of individual savings is certainly acceptable, since Social Security's basic protection is still there regardless of what happens to the individual's investments. But to shift the base itself, or any part of it, to a retirement plan dependent on individual investment decisions seems unwise. . . . It is one thing to have retirement income *supplementary* to Social Security, such as IRAs and 401(k) plans, tied to investments, but quite another thing to have one's basic retirement income dependent on the uncertainties of individual private investment. In that situation, there is more than one kind of risk. In addition to the general risk of picking investments that perform badly, individuals are exposed to the risk of being forced to begin or end an investment period at a bad time. Using projected average investment returns as a basis for retirement planning is

132

treacherous: one can drown in a river with an average depth of six inches and predicted average investment returns will leave some investors destitute and many others with much less income than expected. (ACSS 1997, p. 64)

The six MB members continue as follows.

The Catch in Individual Ownership. Although the intent of the IA plan is to create a nationwide system of individual retirement accounts with the principal and income available only in retirement, it is very doubtful that this objective could be preserved in practice. As with today's IRAs and 401(k) plans, there would be pressure to use individual savings accounts for medical, education, or other needs. If funds go into individually named accounts, as provided for under the IA plan (whose sponsors even argue that the 1.6% wage deduction is not a tax because it continues to be individually owned), account holders will assuredly find it unreasonable to be denied access to their "personal" funds in an emergency – or indeed for any purpose that seems worthwhile. As a result, the total amount that would actually be available for retirement under the IA plan, particularly for low-income people, would almost certainly be far lower than predicted. (pp. 64–5)

Diamond (1997) makes the same point:

Pressures would likely develop to tap individual accounts for other purposes – just as there have been proposals to expand access to IRA funds for nonretirement purposes, such as house purchases and education expenses. While such early access may or may not be seen as good, depending on the perceived need to preserve savings for retirement, it represents a risk for Social Security as a retirement system. Moreover, one could imagine a financially strapped government tapping these accounts by allowing withdrawals as a substitute for government-provided benefits in other programs, for example, unemployment insurance and Medicaid coverage of nursing home expenses. (p. 44)

By contrast, with funded Social Security, there are no individual accounts owned by individual workers. Thus, workers would not press politically to use "their" accounts for other worthwhile purposes because they would not have such accounts.

It is important to recall one of the nine principles of Social Security articulated by advocates of the MB plan but also held by advocates of funded Social Security: partial redistribution from high-wage to low-wage workers through the benefit formula. Individual accounts undermine this principle. Both MB and funded Social Security advocates believe that this principle should govern the distribution of all funds raised for Social Security. As the MB proponents state:

Social Security is a blend of reward for individual effort and, at the same time, perhaps our strongest expression of community solidarity. Social Security is based on the premise that *we're all in this together,* with everyone sharing responsibility not only for contributing to their own and their family's security but also to the security of everyone else, present and future. (ACSS 1997, p. 89)

Funded versus PAYGO with Individual Accounts

Individual accounts are in direct conflict with this fundamental principle of social insurance. The whole point of individual accounts is to let each individual "go it alone" – to do better or worse than fellow retirees because the individual's portfolio outperforms the portfolio of other retirees. This is entirely appropriate for saving outside the social insurance system. Indeed, it can be argued that individual saving for any purpose should be encouraged by tax reform (Seidman 1997). But advocates of both traditional Social Security and funded Social Security believe that the go-it-alone principle has no place in a social insurance program.

In contrast to PSA advocates, IA proponents oppose large-scale privatization. They want the go-it-alone principle to have a limited, restricted place in Social Security. But once individual accounts have been established, will it be politically easy to contain them? IA advocates genuinely hope that, by providing small individual defined-contribution accounts, they can preserve a large role for the defined-benefit plan in Social Security. They see this concession as a strategic retreat that is necessary to undercut momentum for full-scale privatization.

However, it is possible that – despite the intentions of IA advocates – this strategic retreat will turn out to have the opposite effect. Once the administrative apparatus of individual accounts has been established, privatization advocates will correctly point out there is little additional administrative cost in enlarging the accounts; the significant cost comes from the initial establishment of the accounts. Once they are in place, they can be expanded at little cost, so why not expand them? Rather than satisfy the appetite of those who favor the go-it-alone principle, it seems likely that it will merely whet their appetites and provide a new decisive argument: Since we have already

135

incurred the main cost involved in individual accounts – the start-up cost – now let us reap the full benefit.

Moreover, once each individual household has its own account, it is likely that there will be an upsurge of political pressure in favor of the go-it-alone principle. After all, many households would in fact gain by limiting Social Security's partial redistribution from high-wage to low-wage workers. Once they have their accounts and inspect their annual statements, it seems likely that many of these households will press politically for its expansion. Why should these households be satisfied with paying 12.4% to social insurance and only 1.6% to their own accounts?

It is also likely that most households will press for permission to use their own accounts for other urgent purposes (such as medical care, college tuition, or unemployment assistance). If such permission is granted, it will stimulate further pressure to expand the size of the accounts. Such expansion is likely to come at the expense of social insurance. Advocates of account expansion will surely favor diverting part of the 12.4% rather than raising the total tax rate above 14%.

There is no doubt that proponents of the IA plan would strongly oppose such an expansion. After all, they argue against the PSA plan and other forms of privatization. They sincerely believe that the best way to prevent full-scale privatization is to permit a little bit of limited privatization. But they may be incorrect about the political dynamic that will arise from the establishment of individual defined-contribution Social Security accounts. If political momentum builds for expanding the accounts, IA advocates will surely join forces with advocates of the MB plan and funded Social Security in an attempt to hold back the sea of expansion. But politically it may be too late.

136

Funded versus PAYGO with Individual Accounts

Funded Social Security advocates take an alternative, strategic approach to combating large-scale privatization. They accept the judgment that Social Security will become politically vulnerable if it yields a return significantly below low-risk private saving. But rather than acquiesce in the establishment of individual accounts, their strategy is to gradually fund Social Security so that its return will at least match the return on low-risk private saving.

At the same time, advocates of funded Social Security believe that the best way to stop large-scale privatization is to prevent the establishment of any individual defined-contribution Social Security accounts. In their view, this is the strategic point to engage in battle because this is where the forces of privatization are still weak. The high cost of establishing accounts still lies ahead. Households are not yet perusing their annual defined-contribution account statement, wondering why only 1.6% goes to their account while 12.4% goes elsewhere and why they can't use their own account for other urgent purposes.

Thus, advocates of funded Social Security take a hard line against the establishment of individual accounts – not because a permanent 1.6% versus 12.4% split would be intolerable but rather because they believe such a split will prove to be politically unstable. In their view, the most advantageous time to wage a battle against large-scale privatization is prior to the existence of any individual defined-contribution Social Security accounts.

Thus, proponents of the two middle positions – funded Social Security and PAYGO Social Security with supplemental individual accounts – are both opposed to large-scale privatization. But they differ in their assessment of political dynamics. Advocates of supplemental accounts believe that the provision

137

of small-scale, constrained individual accounts is the best way to preserve a large role for defined-benefit Social Security. By contrast, advocates of funded Social Security believe that acquiescing in small-scale accounts would be a fateful strategic error: that the best way to stop privatization is to *prevent* the establishment of any individual Social Security accounts while simultaneously raising the return generated by defined-benefit Social Security through funding.

RECENT PROPOSALS FOR SUPPLEMENTAL
INDIVIDUAL ACCOUNTS

The recent proposals reviewed in this section all keep the payroll tax rate at 12.4% while directing 2 percentage points of the 12.4 points into individual accounts. One crucial question to keep in mind is this: Since the PAYGO system tax rate is cut from 12.4% to 10.4%, how are benefits to be maintained for current retirees?

In the spring of 1998, Senators Moynihan (D-N.Y.) and Kerrey (D-Neb.) proposed: (1) returning Social Security to a PAYGO system by drawing down the Social Security trust fund to pay current benefits; and (2) at the same time giving workers the option of contributing to supplemental individual accounts. From 2001 to 2024, the payroll tax rate would be cut from 12.4% to 10.4%. Beginning in 2025, the tax rate would gradually increase to 13.4% in 2060, and the ceiling would increase automatically in line with the average wage. Starting in 2001, workers would have the option of contributing 2% of payroll to an individual account or keeping 1.0% of payroll as take-home pay.

How are benefits to current retirees to be maintained? Moynihan and Kerrey propose a large increase in the taxable payroll

138

ceiling from $68,400 in 1998 to $97,500 in 2003. Thus, it is incorrect to view this Moynihan–Kerrey proposal as containing a payroll tax cut. Instead, it contains a redistribution of the payroll tax burden away from low- and moderate-income workers (with taxable wages less than $68,400 in 1998) toward high-income workers (with taxable wages greater than $68,400 in 1998). In effect, they propose a tax increase on high-income workers to maintain benefits for current retirees.

For a decade, Moynihan has objected to the burden of the payroll tax on moderate- and low-income workers. His proposal cuts that burden by reducing the tax rate from 12.4% to 10.4% while increasing the burden on high-income workers by raising the ceiling from $68,400 to $97,500 over five years. Moynihan has also asserted that the surplus in Social Security has been used to conceal the deficit in the rest of the budget. His proposal eliminates that annual surplus. If Social Security runs a balanced budget instead of a surplus, the unified budget will show a deficit instead of balance. Moynihan believes that pressure will then be exerted to balance the rest of the budget without the use of payroll taxes.

Advocates of funded Social Security make three comments on the Moynihan–Kerrey proposal. First, raising the ceiling from $68,400 to $97,500 would significantly increase the degree of redistribution implemented by PAYGO Social Security. This might weaken political support for Social Security from many households with labor income above $68,400 and thus intensify their support for privatization. Second, an alternative way to keep the Social Security surplus from concealing the deficit in the rest of the budget is to completely separate Social Security from the federal budget and to require that all official reports on the federal deficit exclude Social Security. Third, while Moynihan and Kerrey want individual accounts to remain subordinate to PAYGO Social Security, others may succeed in expanding the individual accounts at the expense of PAYGO Social Security by (a) further reducing the payroll tax rate and (b) further increasing the percentage of payroll that can be contributed to individual accounts.

In May 1998, The National Commission on Retirement Policy (NCRP), sponsored by the Center for Strategic and International Studies and chaired by Senator Judd (R-N.H.) and Senator Breaux (D-La.), issued a report proposing to refund two percentage points of the current 12.4% OASDI tax into individual savings accounts (ISAs). The proposal is similar to the earlier proposal by Senators Simpson and Kerrey in that the total payroll tax would remain 12.4%; the amount directed into the individual accounts would be 2.0% of payroll instead of 1.6%.

With only 10.4% left for the PAYGO system, how would benefits for current retirees be maintained? Apparently, they would not: the replacement rate (the ratio of the benefit to the previous wage) would be reduced for current retirees. In contrast to the IA plan (which raises the payroll tax rate to 14%) and to the Moynihan–Kerrey plan (which raises the payroll tax on high-income workers through a large increase in the payroll tax ceiling), the NCRP report explicitly rejects any tax increase. The report considers several individual account plans that require an "add-on" above the 12.4% payroll tax rate, but it concludes that this add-on would constitute an unacceptable tax increase.

Thus, the NCRP report recommends that current and future retirees, rather than current taxpayers, bear the burden for establishing new individual accounts for current workers. The prompt cut in the replacement rate is achieved by a variety of means, including reducing the spouse benefit from 50% to 33%, reducing most workers' average indexed monthly earnings (AIME)

140

by using more years to compute the career average, and reducing the benefits that result from a given AIME.

The NCRP report completely ignores the option of funding Social Security. It compares its proposal solely to traditional alternatives such as increasing tax revenues or reducing benefit growth. Unlike the Advisory Council on Social Security (ACSS) report, in which advocates of supplemental individual accounts and of privatization give a detailed critique of funded Social Security, the NCRP report offers no critique. It gives the reader the impression that there are only two options: the traditional approach and supplemental individual accounts.

The NCRP report states that the Thrift Savings Plan (TSP) provides the best model for designing the personal accounts. In order to avoid a prohibitive increase in costs that would harm small employers and the self-employed, this plan assumes that the responsibilities of employers should remain roughly the same as in current law. The report concedes that new individual savings accounts (ISAs) for millions of employees entails added administrative costs and problems. It recommends that the burden of record keeping for each individual be borne by the Social Security Administration and that the administrative costs be distributed proportionally among individual savings accounts.

The essence of individual accounts is individual choice by investors. Like the IA plan, the NCRP report recommends restricting individual choice. Investors could choose among broad-based funds. Gradually, an increased number of investment options would be provided to beneficiaries. The NCRP report concedes that government regulation of private investment firms would be necessary. Investors would have a choice between various government-approved companies to manage funds within the TSP model. The report recommends creation of a comprehensive regulatory program for oversight of asset managers. The NCRP plan envisions more regulation than does the ACSS PSA plan.

Thus, individual choice would be restricted and investment firms would be regulated. So how different is this ISA plan from funded Social Security? One key difference is that this ISA plan is a defined-contribution plan for each person: a person receives a benefit based on the dollars he has contributed and the earnings of his own individual fund. By contrast, funded Social Security is a defined-benefit plan where a person's benefit is based on his wage history according to a legislated formula. Another key difference is that the administrative and regulatory costs required to implement and protect individual accounts are avoided by funded Social Security, because there is no need to keep track of each individual's investment: the Social Security Administration contracts with private firms to manage its portfolio, and each retiree receives a benefit linked to his wage history, not to the performance of a personal investment fund.

Because these individual savings account proposals are modeled on the federal Thrift Savings Fund (TSF), it is especially interesting to read the evaluation of these plans by Francis Cavanaugh (1996), the first executive director and CEO of the Federal Retirement Thrift Investment Board (which manages the TSF). Recall from Chapter 3 that Cavanaugh is a critic of privatization who writes: "Another defect in the privatization option is that it would foolishly shift investment risk from the group (all Social Security participants) to the individual. This violates the fundamental insurance principle of shifting risk from the individual to the group" (p. 104).

After criticizing privatization, Cavanaugh writes:

An alternative approach, proposed by Senators Robert Kerrey (D-Neb.) and Alan Simpson (R-Wyo.), is to offer the 2% privatization option outlined above along with another option that would permit employees to contribute to a 410(k)-type fund like the federal Thrift Savings Fund. The two senators introduced legislation ... in 1995 that would establish (1) in the Social Security Administration (SSA) a Personal Investment Fund Board "in the same manner as the Federal Retirement Thrift Investment Board" and (2) in the Treasury Department a Personal Investment Fund (PIF) "in the same manner as the Thrift Savings Fund." The PIF option would have the potential for certain economies of scale in the consolidation of record keeping, investment management, communication, and other administrative functions. Yet there would remain the perhaps fatal problem of shifting investment risk from the group to risk-averse individuals who probably would not invest enough in the stock market to realize more retirement income than if they had remained in the Social Security system. (p. 106)

Cavanaugh then turns to the administrative aspect of the Kerrey–Simpson plan:

Finally, the administration of any plan as large as the PIF would be a daunting task. With over 2 million participants, the Thrift Savings Plan is the largest defined contribution plan in the country and an enormous administrative challenge. Social Security, with more than 120 million covered employees, is administratively dependent on many millions of employers, including the self-employed, the mom and pop stores, and the households employing part-time maids and nannies earning as little as $1,000 a year – not a seamless operation. If possible at all, it is highly unlikely PIF could ever meet the high fiduciary standards expected of pension plan administrators today. (p. 107)

Thus Cavanaugh, who managed the Thrift Savings Plan for two million participants, is pessimistic about the administrative feasibility of applying the TSP model to 120 million participants. What, then, is his recommendation? Portfolio diversification of the Social Security trust fund. He writes:

The most effective, and perhaps only feasible, way to ensure that Social Security participants are given the stock investment benefits available to virtually all other large retirement plans in the country is to permit the Treasury to invest a large portion, not to exceed 50%, of the Social Security trust fund in a broad stock index fund, such as a S&P 500 or a Wilshire 5000 fund. The investment risk would remain with the group, rather than shift to the individual. There would be no need for expensive individual account maintenance or employee communications program. The administrative costs would be negligible. The entire operation could be managed by a dozen Treasury staff or by a small independent agency to avoid any conflict of interests, compared with a staff perhaps a hundred times larger to administer the PIF or perhaps a thousand times larger to administer the privatization option (including staff of private institutions). This proposal would go a long way toward resolving the long-term Social Security financing problems. (p. 107)

144

WOULD SUPPLEMENTAL INDIVIDUAL ACCOUNTS LEAD TO PRIVATIZATION?

While some support supplemental individual accounts as an alternative to full-scale privatization of Social Security, others believe these accounts are a strategic initial step toward privatization. Just as Milton Friedman supports privatization as a step toward termination of Social Security (see Chapter 3), Martin Feldstein supports supplemental accounts as a step toward privatization.

In a *Wall Street Journal* editorial-page column (November 4, 1997), Feldstein proposes the establishment of personal retirement accounts (PRAs): 2% of the earnings (up to the payroll tax ceiling) of each employee would be sent to a PRA rather than to Social Security. The employee would invest those dollars in stocks, bonds, or mutual funds. In a subsequent article, Feldstein and Samwick (1998) simulate the potential effects of 2% personal retirement accounts. At the beginning of that article, they note that the government might impose regulations requiring, for example, that the funds be invested in diversified mutual funds or bank deposits. Each individual would receive a dollar-for-dollar income tax credit for the amount deposited in a PRA, so the individual would receive a tax cut equal to 2% of earnings on the condition that the tax cut is saved in a personal retirement account.

As we saw in Chapter 3, Feldstein publicly supports the gradual full privatization of Social Security. Evidently, he believes that establishing individual accounts with 2% of earnings would be a strategic initial step. He may be right.

5

Funded versus Means-Tested Social Security

Funded versus Means-Tested Social Security

Means testing is a very different approach to Social Security reform. With means testing, retirees who have sufficient "means" –
income or wealth – would receive little or no Social Security
benefit; the Social Security benefit would be smaller, the higher
the income (or wealth) of the retiree. The report of the Bipartisan
Commission on Entitlement and Tax Reform (1995), created by
President Clinton and headed by Senators Kerrey and Danforth,
gives serious consideration to means testing. Means testing may
be viewed as an alternative to funding Social Security because
each attempts to bring Social Security into long-run financial
balance. A key difference is this: The higher a worker's dollar
wage and payroll tax, the higher is his dollar retirement benefit
with funded Social Security (and current U.S. Social Security),
but the lower is his dollar retirement benefit with means-tested
Social Security.

THE CASE FOR MEANS TESTING SOCIAL SECURITY

Advocates of means testing Social Security assert that Social
Security pays benefits to affluent retirees who "don't need it"
and that the Social Security system can be brought into balance
by reducing benefits to the affluent. From this perspective, a retiree who has sufficient means should receive little or no Social
Security benefit.

One of the commissioners of the Bipartisan Commission on
Entitlement Reform, Peter Peterson, holds this view. In his section of the report, he writes:

> *Enact a comprehensive "affluence test"* .... A cen-
> tral challenge for any entitlement reform plan is how

to achieve large fiscal savings without hurting lower-income Americans. This plan's answer is to institute a comprehensive "affluence test" that would selectively scale back benefit payments to most households with above-median incomes. The test would include all federal benefits: not just Social Security and Medicare, but everything from farm aid to federal pensions. Under the affluence test, households with incomes under $40,000 [in 1995] would not lose a penny in benefits. Higher-income households would lose 10% of all benefits that cause their incomes to exceed $40,000, plus 10% for each additional $10,000 in income. For most types of benefits, the maximum benefit reduction rate would be set at 85%, applicable to household incomes over $120,000 [in 1995] .... (p. 49)

Peterson gives this rationale for affluence testing:

Any reform plan must ask for progressive sacrifice. Our entitlement system – no less than our tax system – should embody the principle of progressivity. Yet when we look at today's entitlement system what we see is a far cry from FDR's original version of a "floor of protection" against destitution. It dispenses most benefits without regard to need. (Three quarters flow through programs that are not means tested.) Although it helps the poor, it does so mostly by dint of the vast sums spent; along the way, it is as likely to shower windfalls on the affluent as on the needy.... It is imperative that the Commission ask for the greatest sacrifice where Federal largess is least deserved – and where the sacrifice will be least burdensome. (p. 54)

Funded versus Means-Tested Social Security

Peterson, the founding president of the Concord Coalition (an organization that advocates tax and expenditure changes to maintain a balanced budget) elaborates in his book (1996). He says that the only way to protect the poor – without deficits or tax increases – is to reduce the entitlements going to the affluent. He asserts that an affluence test is crucial to any reform plan. He emphasizes that his affluence test would affect no household with below-median income, but it would reduce benefits to higher-income households on a steeply progressive basis.

Peterson prefers the term "affluence test" to "means test" because the latter often implies that to receive a benefit the recipient must be poor. Peterson does not propose that Social Security be limited to the poor. Rather, he proposes a reduced Social Security benefit for the middle-income elderly and virtually no benefit for the affluent elderly. Because affluent retirees pay income tax on Social Security benefits, a mild form of affluence testing is already in effect. But Peterson's proposal is much more steeply progressive: the dollar benefit would fall sharply as income rises above the median.

Peterson's proposal is even more redistributive than the first tier of the PSA plan described in Chapter 3. Recall that current Social Security gives a higher benefit to higher wage workers when they retire, though it is less than proportional – a worker with three times the wage might receive twice the benefit. The current defined-benefit formula, which is incorporated in funded Social Security, is thus partially redistributive. The PSA plan's first tier is more redistributive: regardless of wages earned or taxes paid, two retirees with the same years of work receive the same dollar benefit. Peterson's proposal is still more redistributive: under his affluence test, the affluent retiree would receive a smaller dollar benefit than the nonaffluent retiree.

151

It is important to contrast this steeply progressive schedule with the mild implicit schedule that results from the U.S. income tax. For many years, Social Security benefits were exempt from federal income tax. In recent years, the tax code has been amended so that the benefits of affluent retirees are now taxed. But note that, under the income tax, the larger is a retiree's before-tax dollar benefit, the larger is that retiree's after-tax benefit. Thus, the larger is a worker's wage and dollar payroll tax, the larger will be the after-tax dollar benefit when the worker retires. By contrast, with Peterson's steeply progressive schedule, the larger is a worker's wage and dollar payroll tax, the *smaller* will be the after-tax dollar benefit when the worker retires.

To summarize: An affluence test would result in a significant reduction in aggregate Social Security expenditures, and benefits would be cut for relatively affluent retirees.

THE CASE AGAINST MEANS TESTING SOCIAL SECURITY

The MB (maintenance of benefits) advocates on the Advisory Council on Social Security list nine principles they believe should be the foundation of Social Security (we considered these principles at the end of Chapter 3). Two are directly relevant to means testing.

> *Wage-related:* Social Security benefits are related to earnings, thereby reinforcing the concept of benefits as an earned right and recognizing that there is a relationship between one's standard of living while working

152

and the benefit level needed to achieve income security in retirement. Under Social Security, higher-paid earners get higher benefits – while, at the same time, the lower-paid get more for what they pay in . . . .

Not means-tested: In contrast to welfare, eligibility for Social Security does not depend on the beneficiary's current income or assets; nor does the amount of the benefit. This is a crucial principle. It is the absence of a means test that makes it possible for people to add to their savings and to establish private pension plans, secure in the knowledge that they will not be penalized by having their Social Security benefits cut back as a result of having achieved additional retirement income security. The absence of a means test allows Social Security to provide a stable role in anchoring a multi-tier retirement system in which private pensions and personal savings can be built on top of Social Security's basic, defined protection. (ACSS 1997, pp. 95–6)

In their book on Social Security reform, Steuerle and Bakija (1994) provide historical perspective. They explain that the founders of Social Security wanted to help ensure its long-term political survival by giving all participants, regardless of means, a sense of "entitlement" to their promised benefits. They cite a famous quote of President Franklin Roosevelt talking privately to a close advisor:

I guess you're right on the economics, but those taxes were never a problem of economics. They are politics all the way through. We put those payroll contributions there so as to give the contributors a legal, moral, and political right to collect their pensions. . . . With those

153

taxes in there, no damn politician can ever scrap my Social Security program. (p. 26)

Steuerle and Bakija report that the founders of Social Security believed that the absence of means testing was necessary to gain public support because it made Social Security a form of insurance rather than welfare. They quote Wilbur J. Cohen, a former Secretary of Health, Education, and Welfare who for almost five decades played an important role in the evolution of the Social Security system:

> I am convinced that, in the United States, a program that deals only with the poor will end up being a poor program. There is every evidence that this is true. Ever since the Elizabethan Poor Law of 1601, programs only for the poor have been lousy, no good, poor programs. And a program that is only for the poor – one that has nothing in it for the middle income and upper income – is, in the long run, a program the American public won't support. This is why I think one must try to find a way to link the interests of all classes in these programs. (p. 26)

In his classic book on Social Security, Robert Ball, U.S. Commissioner of Social Security from 1962 to 1973 (and one of the six MB members of the ACSS), addresses the issue of means testing. He writes:

> Social insurance is a form of "income insurance," with the benefits designed to make up for a loss of earned income. There is no "means test." Welfare, on the other hand, is a residual program resting on a means test. . . .

154

Funded versus Means-Tested Social Security

In the great majority of social insurance systems the amount of the payment varies with the amount of the earned income lost, so that higher-paid wage earners get larger benefits than lower-paid ones. . . . Many people are very reluctant to apply for welfare, but everyone feels good about applying for Social Security – its theirs; they've earned it . . . . (1978, p. 339)

There seems to me a clear social advantage in relying primarily on an approach that protects incentives to earn and save throughout a working lifetime. . . . From the standpoint of economic incentives, it seems to me important that primary reliance be placed on work-connected payments designed so that the more the individual works, the more he gets. I also think it is important to place primary reliance on payments made without a test of need so that incentives to save and add to the payments made under the basic program are preserved. A means test penalizes the person who saves . . . .

Another important reason why I believe there is a general preference for income insurance is that everyone is included in the same plan, regardless of income. Nobody feels that private insurance and Social Security are only for the "poor" . . . . In income insurance, one part of the community does not take care of another; the community instead provides the instrumentality through which all individuals meet a universal need. Everyone has a stake in his earned social insurance benefits . . . . (pp. 345–6)

In his 1975 article proposing funded Social Security, Martin Feldstein opposed means-testing Social Security:

155

Although Social Security might be replaced by a system of means-tested grants to older persons who have neither the income nor the wealth to be self-sufficient, I believe that this would be a self-defeating policy. If the level of benefits were set high enough to provide what would generally be regarded as an adequate standard of living, the new program would be a substantial incentive to workers not to provide for their old age. The means-tested benefits would thus have the double disadvantage of discouraging savings and lowering the real income of the aged. (p. 88)

Auerbach (1997) makes this comment:

The Concord Coalition, among others, would subject old-age benefits to means-testing .... Such wealth-dependent social insurance would present those who expect to be near the benefit ceiling with a potentially powerful disincentive to save. Those who are fairly certain to be above the ceiling would face no saving disincentive, but would accurately view the payroll tax as not linked to any future benefits. Thus, compared with the present system, means-testing would increase the saving disincentive for some and the labor supply disincentive for others. (p. 72)

In an article entitled "The Folly of Means-Testing Social Security," Burtless (1996) emphasizes the political consequences of means testing. He predicts that affluent workers would strongly resent their Social Security contributions. After all, they would still be taxed on their wages but would now be excluded from benefits. Affluent workers would try to persuade

156

their political representatives to scale back the size of the Social Security program. Although affluent workers and retirees are a minority, experience suggests that their political influence exceeds their numbers. Burtless believes that affluence testing would arouse fierce opposition to Social Security among many affluent workers and would threaten the political consensus that has kept Social Security popular for so long. He contends that an important reason why Social Security receives such high marks from voters is that it is viewed not as a program for the needy but rather as one for all citizens:

> By basing Social Security pensions on retirees' current incomes, means-testing can target benefits more narrowly on people in need, but at a tremendous political cost. The program will be less popular among the affluent and more vulnerable to political attack from ideological opponents of government redistribution.... The ironical result of imposing a means test may be to reduce the amount of income support provided to low-income elderly and disabled Americans. (pp. 179–80)

Kingson and Schulz (1997) directly address Peterson's affluence test, which they call "the new means-testing." They worry that affluence testing would be the first step down a "slippery slope" to full means testing: varying each retiree's benefit inversely with the retiree's income or wealth. They point out that affluence testing can be converted to full means testing simply by reducing the exemption level (Peterson's $40,000). They note that, even without means testing, Social Security's partial redistribution (from high-wage to low-wage workers) makes some high-income workers regard it as a bad deal. Kingson and Schulz fear that affluence testing would push the majority of

157

these workers into political revolt against Social Security and that their hostility would generate strong pressures to permit high-paid workers to opt out of Social Security. They conclude that, in the long run, the greatest losers from affluence testing would be low-income workers, whose decent benefits might be politically unsustainable if middle- and upper-income workers receive little or no Social Security benefits.

6

Questions and Answers

Questions and Answers

Is funding Social Security applicable to most countries?

Yes.

Is funding Social Security a new proposal?

No. This is made clear from citations and quotes throughout this book.

What are the two distinct components of funding Social Security?

Funding Social Security requires: (1) accumulating a large fund by setting taxes and benefits so that Social Security runs substantial annual surpluses; and (2) investing the fund in a diversified portfolio of marketable government securities, corporate bonds, and corporate stocks.

What does each component do?

Fund accumulation is the key to raising the capital accumulation of the economy, whereas portfolio diversification is the key to capturing a larger share of the economy's capital income for the Social Security system. Suppose an increase in the economy's capital accumulation would generate a return to the economy of 6%. Fund accumulation without portfolio diversification would raise capital accumulation (provided the balance in the rest of the government budget is unaltered) and generate a 6% return to the economy. Fund accumulation with portfolio diversification would raise capital accumulation and cause the Social Security system to capture some of this 6% return.

161

Funding Social Security

Is funded Social Security a defined-benefit plan?

Yes. Like the current U.S. Social Security system, funded Social Security is a compulsory, universal, defined-benefit annuity plan with inflation protection: a retiree receives an annual benefit that is tied to the retiree's wage history by a legislated formula, continues for as long as the retiree lives, and is automatically adjusted annually for inflation; moreover, the formula implements partial redistribution from high-wage to low-wage workers.

Does funded Social Security establish any individual accounts?

No. All risk remains pooled.

How does funded Social Security differ from the current U.S. Social Security program?

Solely but crucially in financing. Funded Social Security uses a mix of payroll taxes and portfolio investment income to finance benefits, with an important share contributed by each source. For example, investment income might roughly equal payroll tax revenue in a typical year. By contrast, the current U.S. Social Security program is "pay-as-you-go" (PAYGO): benefits are financed by payroll tax revenues.

Does the government directly manage the portfolio of stocks and bonds?

No. The Social Security Administration contracts with private investment firms (under competitive bidding) to manage the

162

portfolio of the Social Security trust fund; each investment firm manages a share of the trust fund portfolio. Under the contract, each firm must invest its share of the fund in a conservative diversified portfolio of government bonds, corporate bonds, and corporate stocks.

How is this large permanent capital fund accumulated?

This Social Security capital fund is accumulated not by government borrowing but by gradually achieving and maintaining a gap between payroll taxes and benefits during a lengthy transition period. The earned-income tax credit is used to protect low-income workers from the transitional tax burden.

Why invest the Social Security fund in stocks and bonds?

There are three important reasons for investing the portfolio in marketable government securities, corporate bonds, and corporate stocks – rather than in special, nonmarketable government securities (as under the current U.S. Social Security system). First, the yield on the portfolio will be higher. Second, a marketable portfolio will strengthen public confidence that the fund is genuine. Third, a marketable portfolio is less vulnerable to a political raid, because tapping the portfolio involves actual sale of stocks and bonds on the open market.

Is funded Social Security based on an optimistic view of the stock market?

No. History shows that even a conservative diversified stock portfolio can perform poorly over one or even two decades.

Two points should be kept in mind. First, funded Social Security uses portfolio investment income *as well as* payroll taxes to finance benefits; it does not put too many benefit eggs in its portfolio basket. Second, the portfolio is conservative: government bonds constitute an important share of the Social Security portfolio, as do corporate bonds; corporate stocks constitute less than half of the Social Security portfolio.

Does stock market investment imply that Social Security would become a defined-contribution plan?

No. Funded Social Security is a defined-benefit plan, where each retiree's benefit is linked to the retiree's own wage history by a legislative formula. The benefit does not directly depend on the investment performance of the Social Security portfolio.

What happens if the stock market falls?

If portfolio earnings fall, then a fraction of the portfolio must be sold to finance legislated benefits. However, if the portfolio performs poorly for several years, then either the legislative formula must be adjusted or payroll taxes increased. Thus, indirectly, benefits are eventually affected by portfolio performance; funded Social Security does not eliminate stock market risk. But it does minimize the risk for the individual retiree by (a) pooling the risk over all retirees, (b) utilizing a conservative diversified portfolio, (c) spreading the risk over time by selling fund assets as a first resort and adjusting the legislated benefits formula only as a last resort, and (d) using payroll taxes as well as portfolio investment income.

Questions and Answers

Are there two middle positions on Social Security reform?

Yes. There are two middle positions between pay-as-you-go (PAYGO) Social Security and privatized Social Security. One is PAYGO Social Security with supplemental individual defined-contribution accounts. The other is funded Social Security.

Is funded Social Security likely to be a "better deal" than PAYGO Social Security?

Yes. With funded Social Security, the yield depends on the investment income of the Social Security portfolio. The long-term real (inflation-adjusted) return on stocks in the past half century has been estimated to be over 6%. A mixed portfolio of government bonds and corporate stocks and bonds should be able to achieve a real return of 4% with low risk. Economists have shown that the real yield (rate of return) in a mature PAYGO Social Security program will on average equal the growth rate of real output (approximately the sum of labor force and productivity growth). According to most long-term forecasts, this is likely to be about 2% (e.g., perhaps 0% for population growth and 2% for productivity growth).

Is the difference between a 4% and 2% return important?

Yes. This 2% gap makes an enormous difference over a person's lifetime. For example, consider a worker of age 45 saving $5,000 that year. Compounded at 2% per year, this amount grows to $7,430 at age 65; compounded at 4%, it grows to $10,956. Hence, at age 65, the amount is nearly 50% greater ($10,956 / $7,430 = 1.47) when the yield is 4% instead of 2%.

165

Funding Social Security

Is funded Social Security completely different from the three plans proposed in the 1997 Advisory Council on Social Security (ACSS) report?

No. Funded Social Security borrows heavily from all three ACSS plans. Its debt to the authors of these plans is evident throughout the book.

How does funded Social Security differ from the ACSS maintained benefits (MB) plan?

Whereas the MB plan prescribes a small permanent fund, a central feature of funded Social Security is the accumulation of a large permanent fund so that portfolio investment income roughly equals payroll tax revenue. A few individual MB authors may support funding Social Security – the building of a large permanent fund that generates annual investment income comparable to annual payroll tax revenue – but the ACSS MB plan does not call for adjustments in taxes or benefits that would be sufficient to accumulate a large permanent capital fund.

How large would the Social Security fund be?

Here's a rough illustration. Benefits are 5% of GDP. Suppose that, with funded Social Security, investment income is eventually 2% of GDP. If the yield on fund assets is 4%, then fund assets must be 50% of GDP, so the ratio of fund assets to benefits equals ten. Thus, funded Social Security envisions the gradual accumulation of a permanent fund that is roughly ten times annual benefits.

Questions and Answers

How does funded Social Security differ from privatized Social Security?

Privatized Social Security (such as the ACSS personal security accounts plan) prescribes individual defined-contribution accounts that are owned, controlled, and invested by each worker. Funded Social Security is a defined-benefit annuity plan in which the government contracts with private firms to invest its large fund in a broadly diversified portfolio.

How does funded Social Security differ from supplemental individual accounts?

Funded Social Security does *not* introduce individual defined-contribution accounts; rather, it pools all portfolio risk. The introduction of supplemental individual defined-contribution accounts may turn out to be a first step toward privatizing Social Security. If so, Social Security will become much riskier for individuals; if not, Social Security will retain primarily PAYGO financing and yield a lower return than funded Social Security.

Is it important for Social Security to offer a yield comparable to low-risk private saving?

Yes, answer advocates of funded Social Security. In order to politically preserve Social Security as a unified defined-benefit annuity plan with inflation protection and partial redistribution, it may be necessary to gradually change its financing from PAYGO to funding so that, in the future, its yield is comparable to the yield available on low-risk private saving. Hence, funding Social Security is a politically strategic alternative.

167

Funding Social Security

What is an early exposition of the case for funded Social Security?

More than two decades ago, Martin Feldstein of Harvard proposed the conversion of PAYGO Social Security to funded Social Security (Feldstein currently favors privatized Social Security). In his 1975 article (quoted in Chapter 2), he argued that Social Security should set taxes above benefits and accumulate a large fund that would earn investment income to help finance benefits. He contended that changing Social Security's financing would not arouse public hostility as long as Social Security's defined-benefit structure were preserved.

Is it acceptable to raise payroll taxes in the short run in order to accumulate the fund?

Yes, reply advocates of funded Social Security. In his 1975 article, Feldstein argued that if we refuse to raise the payroll tax rate now, we will unfairly burden the next generation by expecting them to pay a much higher tax rate to support us than the rate that we charged ourselves; and if they refuse to pay a much higher tax rate, our benefits will be much smaller than we now expect.

Why not build the fund by borrowing?

Financing the fund accumulation by government borrowing would cancel the positive impact on the national saving rate and capital stock.

Can low-income workers be protected from the payroll tax increase?

Questions and Answers

Yes. An expansion of the earned-income tax credit can protect low-income workers from the transitional burden.

Is the fund built solely by payroll tax increases?

No. Slower benefit growth than currently scheduled will also help accumulate the fund.

Is it possible to avoid a transition cost when the fund is built?

No. Current workers and retirees with moderate and high incomes must share the burden from the initial slower growth in consumption that accompanies the increase in the national saving rate and the accumulation of the fund. Any increase in the saving rate has a transition cost. Although consumption growth can remain positive, below-normal growth entails a short-run sacrifice.

Is it important to raise the national saving rate?

Yes, answer many economists. The current saving rate is not the result of preferences being expressed in an undistorted free market, because saving has been discouraged by two government interventions: (i) the taxation of capital income under the income tax and (ii) PAYGO Social Security.

Should Social Security be excluded from the federal budget that must be balanced?

Yes, reply most Social Security experts and economists. Social Security experts emphasize that Social Security must be

planned over a time horizon of many decades and should therefore be separated from the annual budget cycle. Economists
point out that funding Social Security together with exclusion
from the official budget will raise national saving. Why? The
public favors a balanced budget. Excluding Social Security will
create greater pressure on Congress to balance the rest of the
budget. If it does, then Social Security saving adds to national
saving.

Is it feasible to manage a Social Security portfolio?

Advocates answer, yes. In his 1996 book (quoted in Chapters
2 and 3), Francis Cavanaugh, the first executive director and
CEO of the Federal Retirement Thrift Investment Board, argues
that the recent development of stock index funds provides an
acceptable vehicle for the investment of public funds in private
equity securities. As the first executive director of the Board
(1986–94), he encountered no serious problems in selecting an
index (the S&P 500), obtaining competitive bids from large
index fund managers, and establishing an efficient stock fund
with minimal administrative expenses. Cavanaugh sees no reason why the Social Security trust fund should not have the same
stock investment advantage as the Thrift Savings Plan.

*What is to prevent Congress and the president from raiding the
fund at some future time?*

There are four ways to guard against a raid. First, keep the
Social Security Administration an independent agency. Second, exclude Social Security from the federal budget that must

be balanced. Third, invest in a marketable portfolio of stocks and bonds (instead of in nonmarketable Treasury securities). Fourth, annually send each worker an estimate of her retirement benefit, so that a raid will show up on the annual statement.

What is "privatized" Social Security?

Privatized Social Security is a mandatory defined-contribution plan where all workers are required to contribute to a retirement fund (of their choice), where retirees receive benefits that depend solely on their individual funds' portfolio earnings, and where each person owns and controls such a portfolio and the choice of whether to purchase an annuity upon retirement.

Does privatization involve a transitional burden?

Yes. While current workers must make payments to their own retirement funds, they must continue to pay for benefit obligations to current retirees and current workers (when they retire) who have paid Social Security taxes during their careers. Thus, privatization requires obtaining new revenue – either by a tax increase, government spending cut, or borrowing.

Does privatization shift investment risk to the individual retiree?

Yes. If investment returns fall short of expectations, who bears the risk? With funded Social Security, the risk is shared collectively and is spread across generations. With privatization, each individual bears the risk of his own portfolio.

171

Funding Social Security

What happens if the stock market falls?

With privatized Social Security, many retirees – dependent on their own defined-contribution accounts – would suffer a sharp unexpected cut in their retirement benefits. Each retiree would be on his own. By contrast, with funded Social Security, Congress would be expected to meet its commitment to retirees under its defined-benefit plan. This might require the managers to sell some of the assets in the Social Security portfolio in order to meet commitments.

Can workers satisfactorily manage their own accounts under privatization?

Privatization advocates answer, yes. They say that most people will become informed once they must make investment choices. But this view ignores the likelihood that many adults may prove unable to master the basics of finance and investing. Moreover, aggressive advertising by competing investment firms will generate both accurate and misleading information, making it harder, not easier, for the typical individual to figure out what to do. A central argument for funded Social Security is that it enables the average person to reap the higher expected returns of the stock market without individual risk bearing.

Is funded Social Security simpler to administer than privatized Social Security?

Based on his experience managing the Thrift Saving Plan, Cavanaugh answers yes. He argues that, with funded Social Security, there would be no need for costly individual account maintenance or employee communications programs, and management would require only a small staff. He estimates that a staff

172

"a thousand times larger" would be required to administer privatized Social Security (including staff of private institutions).

Would funded Social Security result in harmful political interference in the private sector?

Advocates of privatization say, yes. They believe it is undesirable for the federal government to become a large investor in private capital markets because the pressures to use the funds for socially or politically desirable goals would be enormous. They foresee tremendous conflicts of interest for the government in its role as fiduciary for Social Security participants, on the one hand, and as regulator of business in the interest of the public welfare, on the other. They predict interference in corporate governance through stock voting.

Advocates of funded Social Security regard these risks as low. They emphasize that funded Social Security prohibits direct selection of particular stocks by personnel of the Social Security Administration, which would instead contract with private investment firms under competitive bidding to manage the portfolio of the Social Security trust fund. Each investment firm would manage a share of the trust fund portfolio, with instructions to manage Social Security's portfolio the way it manages the portfolio of a conservative, risk-averse private client.

Would privatization eventually lead to the termination of Social Security?

It might. Advocates of privatization support universal compulsory Social Security. Nevertheless, since each household owns and controls its defined-contribution retirement fund, it is bound to ask whether it can use its fund for a medical emergency or some other worthy purpose such as financing college or a first home. There is a political risk that individually owned defined-contribution accounts may gradually be converted to multipurpose funds.

What is the supplemental individual accounts plan?

In contrast to privatization, this plan introduces small, restricted, individual defined-contribution accounts but preserves PAYGO Social Security. Its advocates claim several advantages. Individuals choose from a few index funds offered by Social Security, so administrative and sales costs (and individual risk) are less than under privatization. The plan converts fund accumulations to an annuity on retirement that is annually adjusted for inflation. In contrast to funded Social Security, individual accounts decentralize decisions over how the funds are invested; if stocks do not perform up to expectations, individuals can blame their own investment decisions and try to correct them.

Why do advocates of funded Social Security oppose supplemental accounts?

Funded Social Security would eventually yield a return of 4% instead of the 2% projected with PAYGO Social Security. By contrast, supplemental accounts are intended to be a small addition to PAYGO Social Security, so that the return on Social Security would remain near 2%. Funded Social Security pools all portfolio risk, whereas supplemental accounts place the risk on each individual household. Supplemental accounts may not prove to be politically stable, because high earners may press for

174

cuts in PAYGO Social Security to make more funds available for their individual accounts. This could lead to the unraveling of the redistributional provisions of Social Security. It may prove politically difficult to prevent supplemental accounts from being used for worthy purposes other than retirement.

Why is funded Social Security a "strategic alternative" to supplemental accounts?

Both plans are alternatives to privatization. Funded Social Security gradually raises the return of Social Security so that it matches the return on low-risk private saving. Its advocates believe that the politically strategic time to wage a battle against privatization is *prior* to the existence of any individual defined-contribution Social Security accounts. Once individual accounts are established, it may be too late politically to prevent their expansion. Acquiescing in supplemental accounts may prove a fateful strategic error. Just as Milton Friedman supports privatization as a step toward termination of Social Security, Martin Feldstein supports supplemental accounts as a step toward privatization. He may be right.

Should Social Security be means-tested?

Advocates of means testing ("affluence testing") Social Security assert that Social Security pays benefits to affluent retirees who "don't need it" and that the Social Security system can be brought into balance by reducing benefits to the affluent. Opponents point out that current Social Security is partially redistributive: it gives a higher benefit to higher-wage workers when they retire, though it is less than proportional – a worker with three times the wage might receive twice the benefit. With affluence testing, the affluent retiree would receive a smaller dollar benefit or none at all. The affluent would exert pressure to reduce Social Security taxes and benefits, and Social Security might come to be regarded as welfare.

Should funded Social Security retain an earmarked payroll tax?

Advocates answer, yes. Although the investment income from a large permanent capital fund will finance roughly half of benefits, substantial tax revenue will still be necessary. An earmarked payroll tax is psychologically important. President Franklin Roosevelt told a close advisor that an earmarked tax gives workers a moral and political right to collect their pensions, so that "no damn politician" would ever be able to "scrap" Social Security.

Would funded Social Security adhere to the nine principles advocated by supporters of traditional U.S. Social Security?

Yes. The principles are that Social Security should be universal, an earned right, wage-related, contributory and self-financed, redistributive, not means-tested, wage-indexed, inflation-protected, and compulsory. Funded Social Security is a defined-benefit annuity plan with inflation protection and partial redistribution; payment of sufficient earmarked payroll taxes gives each worker a moral and political claim to legislated defined benefits. Funded Social Security differs from current Social Security *solely* in its financing.

Is funding Social Security a strategy for preserving these principles?

176

Advocates answer, yes. Funding Social Security is a politically strategic alternative: the best way to politically protect Social Security embodying these nine principles is to make sure that a unified defined-benefit Social Security offers most workers as good a deal as low-risk private saving. This can be done by (a) accepting the short-term sacrifice required to gradually accumulate a large capital fund and (b) contracting with private firms to invest that fund in a diversified portfolio of stocks and bonds. The portfolio should generate a real return of about 4% (with low risk), compared to the 2% return of PAYGO Social Security.

Would privatized Social Security adhere to all nine of these principles?

No. The principle of partial redistribution from high-wage to low-wage workers through the benefit formula is rejected by most advocates of privatization, who believe that a virtue of privatization is that each person receives the retirement portfolio she has accumulated over her work life, free from redistributions by Congress. Privatized Social Security is a defined-contribution (not a defined-benefit) plan, so a person's benefit is not directly linked to past wages. Privatized Social Security does not guarantee inflation protection.

How do funded and privatized Social Security differ in basic philosophy?

The six MB members of the Advisory Council give a general statement of their philosophy (quoted in Chapter 3), which applies to both current and funded Social Security. They write that

177

Funding Social Security

Social Security rests on the premise that *"we're all in this together,"* with each generation of workers sharing responsibility for each generation of retirees. With each worker's future uncertain, Social Security pools the risk: it implements – at low administrative cost – a partial redistribution from high earners to low earners through its benefit formula.

In summary, what do advocates of funded Social Security recommend?

"Fund it, don't privatize it."

References

Aaron, Henry. 1997. Privatizing Social Security: A Bad Idea Whose Time Will Never Come. *Brookings Review* 15(3): 17–23.

Aaron, Henry J., Barry P. Bosworth, and Gary Burtless. 1989. *Can America Afford to Grow Old?* Washington, DC: Brookings Institution.

Advisory Council on Social Security [ACSS]. 1997. *Report of the 1994–1996 Advisory Council on Social Security. Volume I: Findings and Recommendations.* Washington, DC.

Auerbach, Alan J. 1997. Comment on Macroeconomic Aspects of Social Security Reform by Peter A. Diamond. *Brookings Papers on Economic Activity* 2: 67–73.

Auerbach, Alan J., and Laurence J. Kotlikoff. 1987. *Dynamic Fiscal Policy.* New York: Cambridge University Press.

Ball, Robert M. 1978. *Social Security Today and Tomorrow.* New York: Columbia University Press.

Ball, Robert M., with Thomas N. Bethell. 1997. Bridging the Centuries: The Case for Traditional Social Security. In Eric R. Kingson and James H. Schulz (Eds.), *Social Security in the 21st Century,* pp. 259–94. New York: Oxford University Press.

Bipartisan Commission on Entitlement and Tax Reform. 1995. *Final Report of the Bipartisan Commission on Entitlement and Tax Reform.* Washington, DC.

179

References

Board of Trustees, Federal Old-Age and Survivors Insurance and Disability Insurance Trust Fund. *1998 Annual Report of the Board of Trustees of the Federal Old-Age and Survivors Insurance and Disability Insurance Trust Fund.* Washington, DC.

Boskin, Michael J. 1986. *Too Many Promises: The Uncertain Future of Social Security.* Homewood, IL: Dow Jones–Irwin.

Bosworth, Barry. 1996. Fund Accumulation: How Much? How Managed? In Peter Diamond, David Lindeman, and Howard Young (Eds.), *Social Security: What Role for the Future?,* pp. 89–115. Washington, DC: National Academy of Social Insurance.

Burtless, Gary. 1996. The Folly of Means-Testing Social Security. In Peter Diamond, David Lindeman, and Howard Young (Eds.), *Social Security: What Role for the Future?,* pp. 172–80. Washington, DC: National Academy of Social Insurance.

Cavanaugh, Francis. 1996. *The Truth About the National Debt.* Boston: Harvard Business School Press.

Diamond, Peter. 1996a. The Future of Social Security. In Peter Diamond, David Lindeman, and Howard Young (Eds.), *Social Security: What Role for the Future?,* pp. 225–33. Washington, DC: National Academy of Social Insurance.

1996b. Proposals to Restructure Social Security. *Journal of Economic Perspectives* 10(3): 67–88.

1997. Macroeconomic Aspects of Social Security Reform. *Brookings Papers on Economic Activity* 2: 1–66.

Feldstein, Martin. 1975. Toward a Reform of Social Security. *Public Interest* 40: 75–95.

1996. The Missing Piece in Policy Analysis. *American Economic Review Papers and Proceedings* 86(2): 1–14.

1997. Don't Waste the Budget Surplus. *The Wall Street Journal* (4 November): A22.

1998. A New Era of Social Security. *Public Interest* 130: 102–25.

References

Feldstein, Martin, Louis Dicks-Mireaux, and James Poterba. 1983. The Effective Tax Rate and the Pretax Rate of Return. *Journal of Public Economics* 21(2): 129–58.

Feldstein, Martin, and Andrew Samwick. 1997. The Economics of Prefunding Social Security and Medicare Benefits. In Ben Bernanke and Julio Rotemberg (Eds.), *NBER Macroeconomics Annual 1997,* pp. 115–48. Cambridge, MA: MIT Press.

1998. Potential Effects of Two Percent Personal Retirement Accounts. *Tax Notes* 79(5): 615–20.

Ferrara, Peter J. 1982. *Social Security: Averting the Crisis.* Washington, DC: Cato Institute.

1997. A Plan for Privatizing Social Security. SSP no. 8, April 30, Cato Institute, Washington, DC.

Friedland, Jonathan. 1997. Chile's Celebrated Pension-Fund System Has Growing Pains as Returns Decline. *The Wall Street Journal* (12 August): A10.

Friedman, Milton, and Rose Friedman. 1980. *Free to Choose: A Personal Statement.* New York: Avon.

Geanakoplos, John, Olivia S. Mitchell, and Stephen P. Zeldes. 1999. Social Security's Money's Worth. In Olivia S. Mitchell, Robert J. Myers, and Howard Young (Eds.), *Prospects for Social Security Reform.* Pension Research Council and University of Pennsylvania Press.

Gramlich, Edward M. 1996. Different Approaches for Dealing with Social Security. *Journal of Economic Perspectives* 10(3): 55–66.

Kingson, Eric R., and James H. Schulz. 1997. Should Social Security Be Means-Tested? In Eric R. Kingson and James H. Schulz (Eds.), *Social Security in the 21st Century,* pp. 41–61. New York: Oxford University Press.

Kotklikoff, Laurence J. 1996. Privatizing Social Security: How It Works and Why It Matters. In James M. Poterba (Ed.), *Tax Policy and the Economy 10,* pp. 1–32. Cambridge, MA: MIT Press.

References

Kotlikoff, Laurence J., Kent A. Smetters, and Jan Walliser. 1998. Social Security: Privatization and Progressivity. *American Economic Review Papers and Proceedings* 88(2): 137–41.

Kotlikoff, Laurence J., and Jeffrey Sachs. 1997. Privatizing Social Security: It's High Time to Privatize. *Brookings Review* 15(3): 16–22.

Mitchell, Olivia S., and Stephen P. Zeldes. 1996. Social Security Privatization: A Structure for Analysis. *American Economic Review* 86(2): 363–7.

Munnell, Alicia H. 1977. *The Future of Social Security.* Washington, DC: Brookings Institution.

Myers, Robert J. 1993. *Social Security,* 4th ed. Philadelphia: University of Pennsylvania Press.

National Commission on Retirement Policy. 1998. *The 21st Century Retirement Security Plan.* Washington, DC: Center for Strategic and International Studies.

Peterson, Peter G. 1996. *Will America Grow Up Before It Grows Old?* New York: Random House.

Poterba, James, and Andrew Samwick. 1995. Stock Ownership Patterns, Stock Market Fluctuations, and Consumption. *Brookings Papers on Economic Activity* 2: 295–357.

Quinn, Joseph F., and Olivia S. Mitchell. 1996. Social Security on the Table. *American Prospect* (May/June): 76–81.

Rippe, Richard. 1995. Further Gains in Corporate Profitability. *Economic Outlook Monthly,* no. 95-3307 (August), Prudential Securities, Inc., New York.

Seidman, Laurence S. 1983. Social Security and Demographics in a Life-Cycle Growth Model. *National Tax Journal* 36(2): 213–24.

——— 1986. A Phase-Down of Social Security: The Transition in a Life-Cycle Growth Model. *National Tax Journal* 39(1): 97–107.

——— 1997. *The USA Tax: A Progressive Consumption Tax.* Cambridge, MA: MIT Press.

References

1998a. The Case for Funding Social Security. *Public Interest* 130: 93–101.

1998b. *Economic Parables and Policies.* Armonk, NY: M. E. Sharpe.

1998c. Funding Social Security. *Tax Notes* 80(15): 241–9.

Seidman, Laurence S., and Kenneth A. Lewis. 1998. Funding Social Security: The Transition in a Life-Cycle Growth Model. Working Paper, Department of Economics, University of Delaware, Newark.

Seidman, Laurence S., and Brian Westenbroek. 1998. Social Security Fund Accumulation. Working Paper, Department of Economics, University of Delaware, Newark.

Siegel, Jeremy J. 1994. *Stocks for the Long Run.* Burr Ridge, IL: Irwin.

Steuerle, C. Eugene, and Jon M. Bakija. 1994. *Retooling Social Security for the 21st Century.* Washington, DC: Urban Institute Press.

U.S. Congressional Budget Office. 1998. Social Security Privatization and the Annuities Market. *CBO Papers* (February): 1–33.

U.S. General Accounting Office. 1998. *Social Security Financing: Implications of Government Stock Investing for the Trust Fund, the Federal Budget, and the Economy.* Washington, DC.

World Bank. 1994. *Averting the Old Age Crisis.* New York: Oxford University Press.

Index

185

Index

Index

Index

DATE DUE

DEC 2 2 2000			
FEB 0 6 2001			
AUG 1 1 2001			
JUL 1 6 REC'D			
OCT 2 4 2005			
NOV 1 9 REC'D			
DEC 1 0 2007			
NOV 2 9 REC'D			
MAY 0 7 2010			
MAY 0 4 REC'D			
OCT 2 9 2010			
GAYLORD			PRINTED IN U.S.A.